The Conure Handbook

Anne C. Watkins

Filled with Full-color Photographs
Illustrations by Michele Earle-Bridges

BARRON'S

Dedication

To my family, with much love: Allen, Laura and John, Bailey, Chelsea, and Tyler. Special thanks to Rio, my forever friend, *Philippians 4:13*.

About the the Author

In addition to being an expert on conures, Anne Watkins has published widely on a variety of subjects, ranging from parrots to health issues. Her work has appeared in such periodicals as *Pet Age Magazine*. *The Conure Handbook* is her first book for Barron's.

Cover Photos

Norvia Behling: front cover; Gerry Bucsis and Barbara Somerville: front cover and inside front cover; Isabelle Francais: front cover; and B. Everett Webb: front cover, back cover, and inside back cover.

Photo Credits

Bob and Jessie Abbot: pages 30 and 123; Norvia Behling: pages 25 (bottom), 37, 50, 52, 54, 55, 57, 58, 63, 78, 84, 117, 127, 132, and 153; Gerry Bucsis and Barbara Somerville: pages 20, 25 (top), 26, 110, 116, 120, 125, 141, and 144; G. Ebben: pages 14, 128, and 129; Isabelle Francais: pages 3, 16, 19, 22, 38 (left), 39 (top and bottom), 59, 60, 76, 85, 89, 90, 91 (left), 109, 111, 119, 134, 138, 139, 146, and 148; F. Mertens: page 42; Connie Summers: pages 6, 81, 83, 91 (right), 92 (top), 100, 113, 142, and 143; P. van der Hooven: pages 12, 27, 147, 149, and 152; B. Everett Webb: pages vi, 4, 5, 7, 8, 11 (top and bottom), 13, 17, 18, 23, 33, 34, 38 (right), 44, 46, 53, 74, 82, 87, 92 (bottom), 96, 98, 99, 114, 118, 131, and 137.

All inquiries should be addressed to:
Barron's Educational Series, Inc.
250 Wireless Boulevard
Hauppauge, New York 11788
http://www.barronseduc.com

ISBN-13: 978-0-7641-2783-0
ISBN-10: 0-7641-2783-7

Library of Congress Catalog Card No. 2003068841

Library of Congress Cataloging-in-Publication Data

Watkins, Anne C.
    The conure handbook / Anne C. Watkins.
        p.   cm.
    Includes bibliographical references (p.).
    ISBN 0-7641-2783-7 (alk. paper)
        1. Conures. I. Title.

SF473.C65W38 2004
636.6'865—dc22   2003068841

Printed in China
9 8 7 6

Important Note

Poorly socialized or unhealthy conures may be a danger to humans in the household. If you are bitten or scratched by your conure, you should consult your physician immediately.

Escaped non-native species may represent an environmental threat in some places. Outdoor release or unrestricted outdoor flight is absolutely condemned by the ethical conure keeper. This book recommends that a conure's wing feathers be carefully trimmed at regular intervals.

Contents

Chapter One

What Are Conures?

Beautiful. Charming. Curious. Intelligent. Interactive. Messy. Stubborn. What in the world do all these words have in common? Spend some time with a conure and you'll find out! These comical little parrots have lots to offer anyone wanting a personable bird that will become a treasured member of the family. Conures aren't too big, they don't require the huge setups needed by many of the larger parrots, and they can learn to talk and do tricks. And with so many different species available, you should be able to find a conure that will fit your budget and living situation.

An Introduction to Conures

Conures in the wild can be found in Central America, Mexico, South America, and many of the Caribbean Islands. They often live and travel in flocks, and their natural habitats

Green-cheeked conure.

cover a wide range of areas, including jungles, mountains, rain forests, and farmland.

Once plentiful, now some conures are considered endangered. Deforestation of their native habitats, the increasing need for agricultural areas, and heavy trapping for the pet trade took serious tolls on their numbers. Parrot importation stopped around 1992, so the only wild-caught conures you will find today entered the country many years ago. Fortunately, a lot of those imported conures were set up for breeding, making high-quality, domestically bred conures easy to find.

General Description

All conures have several common characteristics that make them easy to identify. They have long, pointed tail feathers and hooked bills, and they all have bands of featherless skin, called periophthalmic rings, around the eyes. These eye rings can range in color from bright white to grayish to shades of red, depending on the species. Like other psittacines (parrot-type birds), conures are zygodactylous, which means that each foot has two toes pointing forward and two toes that point backward. Conure bodies are slender and streamlined with the exception of some of the smaller species, which may be chunkier but will still have the long line typical of the conure body.

Conures in the Wild

In their native habitats, most wild conures prefer very similar diets, which consist primarily of seeds and berries, fruits and nuts, vegetation, and various types of bugs and larvae. They also tend to forage in agricultural areas, a habit that has made them unwelcome to farmers. Many species exhibit similar behaviors; they are avid chewers, active climbers, and very vocal. Some also enjoy bathing and will often use any available water sources as bathtubs.

Besides obvious similarities in coloring and body shape, some types of conures have comparable breeding habits and behavior patterns. Some species nest only in hollows in rocky areas, or in holes in the sides of cliffs. Others prefer to build their nests in the hollows of decaying trees, or in holes left by woodpeckers. There are even some species of conures that will go to nest only if there are arboreal termites in the area.

There is an interesting sense of cooperation between these conures and the tree-dwelling termites. After the conures dig a cavity into the paperlike termite nest and lay their eggs inside, the termites seal off their section of the nest from that of the conures. Then the termites and conures live together peacefully. When the conures and their young abandon the nest, the termites fill in the cavity and go on about their business.

Types of Conures

There are five main groups of conures. Some of them are so similar that they can be easily confused for the other. All have the potential for becoming great pets, and owners of each species will argue that their conure is the best.

The largest group of conures are the *Aratingas*. *Aratinga* conures are so named because of their similarity to macaws, both in body shape and behavior. Macaws are of the genus *Ara*. "Tinga" is a diminutive. Put the two words together and you have *Aratinga*, which literally means "little macaw."

Size-wise, they are some of the biggest conures, and they have voices to match their bodies. Though they are loud and extremely active birds, many also enjoy cuddling with their favorite humans. Some of the more commonly seen *Aratingas* are the Sharp-tailed conure or the Blue-crowned conure, the Sun conure, the

Jenday conure, the Mitred conure, and the White-eyed conure. The Red-throated and the Brown-throated conures, the Finsch's conure, and the Dusky-headed conure are all equally attractive, but can be harder to find. Special federal permits are required to own the endangered Queen of Bavaria, or Golden, conure.

The smaller *Pyrrhuras* are much quieter than the larger conures, not as destructive with their chewing, and are every bit as outgoing and active as the bigger birds. These personable conures are compact in size, have chunkier bodies, and some are not much bigger than lovebirds. Though their voices are a bit hoarser than the other conures, some can learn to talk in an understandable tone. Unfortunately, some of them aren't as easy to find on the market as other species of conures. Included in this genus are the popular Green-cheeked conure and the Maroon-bellied conure, the Painted conure, the Crimson-bellied conure, and the White-eared conure. Maroon-bellied conures and Green-cheeked conures are usually easier to find than most conures of the *Pyrrhura* genus.

There are also the "other" conures: Patagonian conures, of the genus *Cyanoliseus,* are the largest conures of all. Their eye rings narrow to a point behind their eyes, giving them an exotic appearance, and their voices are extremely loud and penetrating. Roughly 17 inches to 18 inches (43–45 cm) in size, these large birds are becoming more popular as pets, have friendly, curious

Sun conure snuggling with a Green-cheek.

personalities, and can learn to talk. Hand-fed babies are available.

The unusual-looking Slender-billed conure and the Austral conure are members of the genus *Enicognathus.* Also South American parrots, they are native primarily to Argentina and Chile. While not found in great numbers in the pet trade, they are becoming more popular.

The only conure in the genus *Nandayus* is the Nanday conure. These friendly parrots love attention and are beautiful in appearance. Unfortunately, Nandays have earned a reputation for being screechers. Their harsh vocalizations can sometimes make them seem undesirable as pets, but they can become tame and loving companions.

Blue-crowned conure.

Conures as Pets

Often considered the next step up for the person desiring a large parrot, conures have "big bird" personalities packed into small bodies. Less expensive than the larger parrots but every bit as exciting and intelligent, companion conures have so much to offer that you may decide you don't need that bigger parrot after all.

With so many species of conures to choose from, it is important to take time to learn as much about them as possible before making a final selection. Visit pet stores and conure breeders. Read conure books and bird magazines. Study pictures of different types of conures and compare their appearances and sizes. Research conures on the Internet, or join an on-line conure discussion group where you can ask experienced conure keepers lots of questions.

Is a Conure Right for You?

Conures are outgoing, opinionated creatures that enjoy being in the middle of every family activity.

4

They like to add their comments and observations to any conversation, and they consider their human companions to be parts of their flock, and not the other way around. Social and curious, conures insist on being included in each part of day-to-day family life and will suffer if kept shut away in a back room and ignored. Depending on the species and the care your conure receives, a well-cared-for pet conure can live up to 20 to 35 years or more. The conure you choose today could be your avian companion for many years to come. If you have the time and energy to devote to one of these smart little birds, then maybe a conure is the right choice for you.

Do Your Homework

If you know someone who has a conure, pay them a visit and watch them interact with the bird. It shouldn't take long for you to realize that conures can be very loud. Breeders, retailers, and hobbyists all agree that conures generate a lot of noise! Singly kept conures aren't as loud, but groups of conures will definitely make themselves heard. Think about this before you decide to adopt more than one conure.

Notice how the conure climbs around in the cage or on the playstand. Conures use their feet to handle toys and food the same way larger parrots do. A healthy conure is very active, and usually the only time it is still is when it is resting or sleeping. Are you prepared to deal with a bird that is always busy?

Green-cheeked conure.

Conures are also messy. They like to shred paper, throw food, and chew up toys, and they defecate a lot. Cages with seed catchers help contain some of the mess, but busy conures will always find ways to spread the mess around. Do you have the patience for constant cleaning?

Personality Plus

In their minds, conures are the mightiest of all birds and they're always ready to prove it. And you should never underestimate the intelligence of these little parrots; you might like to think that you're making the decision to adopt a conure, when in reality the conure has already chosen you and is charming you into adopting it.

Hand-fed baby conures of various species bond readily with their human families, can be taught simple tricks, and many learn to speak. Sometimes you will be able to select your baby conure while it's still being hand-fed.

Before Bringing Your Conure Home

These active, social birds require lots of attention, a good diet, a roomy cage, safe toys, and lots of supervised play time. It is important to take into consideration their previously mentioned ability to screech, and screech loudly—conures are fabulous watch birds and will alert you to anything out of the ordinary. Alarmed conures can and will let loose ear-splitting screams if something startles them, and sometimes they screech just because they feel like it.

Durable toys, playgyms or playstands, and safe, chewable items are necessities for conures. They thrive on exercise and freedom, so plan to provide adequate, supervised out-of-the-cage time every day. Sometimes, bored or depressed conures pluck or chew their feathers. Those destructive habits can be difficult to break once they get started. All conures need and should be given toys and activities that stimulate and challenge them mentally.

A friendly Green-cheek.

Living with a Conure

You may find that living with a conure is a lot like living with a young child. These curious little parrots enjoy exploring and getting into everything they're supposed to stay away from. They're often too adventuresome for their own good, and you have to be prepared to stay one step ahead of them at all times.

They are strong-willed birds and each has its own distinct personality. The amount of handling it allows will depend on the individual conure. Many will be "cuddle birds" that love

Nanday conure.

to snuggle in your hands. A lot of conures enjoy rolling and tumbling around on their favorite human's laps, and some even learn to lie on their backs in the hands of their human companions.

But not every conure, even one that is hand-fed, is willing to be handled. Some parrots never enjoy having their feathers touched, but they can still make wonderful, affectionate pets. Respect your conure's feelings, and be patient and understanding. You may be pleasantly surprised one day to discover that your conure has learned to trust you enough to allow handling and caressing.

Since loudness is a permanent part of the conure makeup, be prepared to allow your conure a certain amount of joyful screeching and squawking every day. Don't let it get out of hand, but don't try to force a normally vocal creature to be quiet all the time. Encourage your conure to direct some of its vocal energy to learning to speak. Imagine how much fun it will be to hear your feathered friend call your name.

A Special Part of the Family

Adopt a conure, bond with it, and you'll have a loyal friend. Always willing and eager to take part in whatever activities are going on at the moment, conures enjoy watching movies, playing games, listening to music and bouncing to the rhythm, singing, and sharing snacks with their human friends. After a while, you'll wonder what you ever did without a conure in your life.

Chapter Two
Species Profiles

Understanding Genus and Species

A genus is a group of animals or plants with common characteristics. There are usually several species within a genus, and some members of a species differ only in minor details from the others in the genus. In the case of conures, many species and subspecies look almost alike, with the exception of a few differently colored feathers.

Each genus of conure is assigned a Latin name. Following the Latin genus name are the Latin species and subspecies names. For example, the Mitred conure's Latin, or scientific, name is *Aratinga* (genus) *mitrata* (species).

The most commonly seen conures in the pet trade are the *Aratinga* and *Pyrrhura* conures. Closely following are the *Nandayus,* or Nanday conures, with the *Cyanoliseus*, or Patagonian conures, gaining in popularity.

Mitred conures snuggling on a perch.

Conures of the Genus *Aratinga*

These birds are the most readily available conures on the market, due to the fact that there are so many species within the genus. Many *Aratinga* conures look very much alike, and all have in common the long, slender *Aratinga* body shape. Coloration varies from species to species. Some birds have a lot of red feathers, usually around the head and neck area, while some are predominantly green. There are those with lots of yellow, orange, and blue feathers, and some at first glance appear to be dull. Upon closer examination, those conures prove to have brilliant iridescent greens and blues in their coloring.

All *Aratinga* conures have outstanding pet qualities, are curious and intelligent, and enjoy playing, bathing, chewing, and climbing. Most can learn to say a few words, and some become very skilled talkers. In the pet trade, some of the most commonly found *Aratinga*

Hybrids and Mutations

In the wild, conures breed only within their own species, but some hobbyists or breeders allow, and even encourage, different conure species to interbreed in captivity. The resulting birds are called hybrids. These hybrid conures also can breed, and will produce young that are yet another step removed from the pure gene pool of the original species. With the decline of wild conures in some of their native habitats, preserving pure bloodlines is important to ensure the future of these conures.

One example of a hybrid conure is the Sunday. This is a cross between a Sun conure and a Jenday conure, and would not occur naturally in the wild. It can be difficult to determine what species some hybrids are, and sometimes they may be passed off as pure species. If you have doubts about the species of any conure you may be interested in, have an avian veterinarian look at it before you buy it.

Mutations are naturally occurring color variations within a species and may show up in domestically bred conures, or in conures in their native habitats. Unfortunately, some wild mutations are in danger from predators because their unusual coloring may attract attention.

Domestically bred mutations can be intensified by linebreeding, or breeding similarly colored conures of the same species. A couple of examples of color mutations are Cinnamon (fallow) Green-cheeked and Yellow-sided Green-cheeked conures. These beautiful conures are pure-blooded and are not to be confused with hybrids.

conures are the Blue-crowned, Dusky-headed, Finsch's, Gold-capped, Jenday, Mitred, Peach-fronted, Red-fronted, and Sun.

Blue-crowned Conures

Distribution: Argentina, Bolivia, Brazil, Colombia, Uruguay, and Venezuela.

Some people believe that the Blue-crowned conure (*Aratinga a. acuticaudata*) is the most intelligent of all conures. Also identified as the Sharp-tailed conure, it is not as brightly colored as many others in the genus *Aratinga,* but it has a quiet beauty that has won it many admirers. The movie *Paulie* brought a brief surge of attention to Blue-crowns because the star of the film was a very gregarious Blue-crowned conure.

The voices of these conures can be loud, but if kept as single pets, they can be taught not to screech as frequently. They usually reach a size of about 15 inches (38 cm) in length, from the top of the head to the tip of the tail feathers. Blue-crowns are successfully raised by domestic breeders, and hand-fed babies make ideal pets. Some breeders and hobbyists have compared their personalities to those of macaws.

The coloration of Blue-crowns consists of green bodies with pale to dusky blue head feathers. In some specimens, the feathers on the back of the head may have a maroon tint to the edges. The flight feathers are mostly green, with touches of dark blue. Their tail feathers are mostly green, with shades of red on the undersides. The irises are orange with black pupils, and the featherless eye ring is white. The upper mandible (beak) is horn colored, with a black lower mandible. For some reason, the upper mandible, or maxilla, tends to grow to a sharp point in some Blue-crowns. The feet are pinkish with dark toenails. Subspecies in the genus are the *Aratinga a. haemorrhous*, the *Aratinga a. neumanni*, the *Aratinga a. koenigi*, and the *Aratinga a. neoxena*. Some of the subspecies may have both top and bottom mandibles that are horn colored.

Cactus Conures

Distribution: Brazil.

The Cactus conure (*Aratinga cactorum*) has a mostly green body, with shades of brown on the forehead, face, throat, and upper chest. The crown (top of the head) has a slight slate blue tint. It has orange feathers on the belly, with some blue on the back of the head and flight feathers, and green tail feathers with a slight amount of blue. The irises are orange and the eye ring is white.

Blue-crowns are friendly, intelligent conures.

The upper mandible is horn colored, while the bottom is gray, and the feet are also gray. Cactus conures measure about 10 inches (25 cm) in

Cactus conure.

length. Very little is known of the breeding habits in the wild of these medium-sized *Aratinga* conures. They have reproduced successfully in captivity and the hand-fed babies are said to make excellent pets.

Cuban Conures
Distribution: Cuba.

The 10-inch (25-cm) Cuban conure (*Aratinga euops*) is mostly green, with a few red feathers sprinkled about the head, nape, and breast. Some red feathers are also found on the thighs and in the wing bends, the edges of the wing feathers are red, and the flight and tail feathers are green with touches of red. The eye ring is whitish and the eyes have yellow irises, while the hooked bill is horn colored. The feet are tan.

In the native habitat of this aptly named conure, large flocks could once be found, but due to deforestation and the destruction of their native habitat, as well as being heavily trapped for trade, these conures are now rarely seen. Captive breeding has been successfully accomplished, but since not many of this species are kept, the babies can be hard to find.

Dusky-headed Conures
Distribution: Brazil, Colombia, Ecuador, and Peru.

The Dusky-headed conure (*Aratinga weddellii*) is mostly green, with a greenish yellow tint on the abdomen, and the head is a soft brownish gray color with blue edges to the feathers. Duskies have a wider eye ring than most conures. They have black mandibles and the feet are gray. There is an olive green hue to the breast, and the primary wing feathers are black with blue edges, while the other wing feathers are green with blue edges. The tail feathers are dark blue on top, with black underneath. This conure is approximately 11 inches (28 cm) long.

The wild Dusky-headed conure sometimes seeks out arboreal termite mounds for nesting sites. Domestic breeders report that this conure is a prolific breeder, and has no set time of the year for breeding. Hand-fed Dusky-headed conures are said to have loving personalities and make sweet, engaging pets.

Dusky-headed conure.

Finsch's Conures

Distribution: Costa Rica, Nicaragua, and Panama.

The *Aratinga finschi,* or Finsch's conure, is mostly green in color, with a yellow-green chest, red forehead, lores (the area over the nostrils), and crown, red at the bends and edges of the wings, and the flight feathers and tail are a yellowish green to olive green. The eye ring is white and the irises are orange, while the mandibles are horn colored. The feet are a light to grayish color. This conure measures about 11 inches (28 cm) in length.

Not considered endangered, they are common in their natural habitat, where they can be found in either small groups or sometimes in flocks numbering in the hundreds. They are not considered difficult to breed in captivity.

Gold-capped Conures

Distribution: Brazil.

The Gold-cap (*Aratinga auricapilla*) is described as having a friendly, affectionate personality. Said to make good pets, these 12-inch-long (30-cm) birds are colorful and hardy. Their main color is green, but they have orange feathering on their forehead and face that turns to brighter yellow toward the crown and the back of the head. Their bellies have variegated orange and red feathers, the wing feathers are green, edged in blue, and the tail is dark green. The iris is brown, surrounded by a white eye ring. Mandibles are black, as are the feet. Subspecies *Aratinga a.*

A pretty Gold-capped conure.

aurifrons, the Golden-fronted conure, is the same size, but is slightly darker in appearance with more green on the face.

In the wild, Gold-caps make their homes in whatever forested areas are available, and live in small groups. Their coloring makes it easy for them to hide in foliage. Due to heavy deforestation and construction, much of the natural habitat of these conures has been destroyed. Considered rare and endangered, captive breeding of this species is encouraged. Not much is known about their natural diet, or about their breeding or behavior in the wild, but breeding in avicultural setups has been accomplished successfully. Hand-fed babies are often available.

Golden Conures

Distribution: The rain forest canopy of Brazil.

The Golden conure (*Aratinga guarouba*) is a visually impressive bird. Also called the Queen of Bavaria conure, its body is a rich, golden yellow. It has green flight feathers, horn-colored mandibles, and pinkish feet. The eye ring is white and the irises are brown. Young birds are pale green, with their adult coloration coming in when they are around two years old. An adult Golden conure measures about 13.5 inches (34 cm) in length. This conure has recently been designated the genus of *Guaruba guarouba*.

The Queen of Bavaria, or Golden, conure.

Due to deforestation and to being heavily trapped for trade, their status is listed as endangered. They are seen only rarely in their native habitat, and are also uncommon in captivity. Their situation is so serious that in order to obtain one of these birds in the United States, it is necessary to have a Captive-Bred Endangered Species Permit issued by the U.S. Fish and Wildlife Service. This permit is issued only with the understanding that the conures will be allowed to reproduce if a suitable breeding situation can be arranged, and that the birds be housed, maintained, and kept in the healthiest conditions possible.

Green Conures

Distribution: Southern and eastern Mexico, parts of Nicaragua.

The Green conure (*Aratinga h. holochlora*) is a mostly green bird, with a yellowish green tint to its breast and abdomen area. Some birds have a few red head and chest feathers, while others have no red at all. Wing and tail feathers have yellowish green and olive casts, with some olive-yellow washes. The eye ring is a dull reddish gray, and the eyes are orange to reddish. The mandible is horn colored with dark markings. The feet are light colored and the body size tip to tip is roughly 12.5 inches (32 cm) in length.

Others in the Green conure group are the Brewster's Green conure (*Aratinga h. brewsteri*), which is darker than the Green conure, with less yellow, and the crown has a slight blue tint. The Nicaraguan Green conure (*Aratinga h. strenua*) is larger body-wise, and has bigger mandibles, while the Socorro Green conure (*Aratinga h. brevipes*) has darker colors and a longer tail than other Green conures. Subspecies *Aratinga h. rubritorquis,* the Red-throated conure, is green with orange-red feathers on the throat and breast.

Green conures are sometimes considered to be pests to farmers because of the damage they do to crops. Besides the grain pilfered from fields, they eat seeds, berries, nuts, fruits, and vegetation. These noisy conures enjoy chewing and bathing, and nest in tree hollows and crevices in abandoned buildings. Sometimes they will nest in arboreal termite mounds, and they can be difficult to breed in captivity.

Hispaniolan Conures

Distribution: The Island of His-paniola.

Featuring mostly green feather-ing, the Hispaniolan conure (*Aratinga chloroptera*) will sometimes have a red feather or two on its head. Wing bends and feather edges are red, while the undersides of flight feath-ers and tail feathers are green. The amount of red varies from specimen to specimen. The eye ring is white and the irises are brown. With gray feet and a horn-colored bill, the His-paniolan conure measures about 12.5 inches (32 cm).

Also in this group is the Puerto Rican conure, or Mauge's conure (*Aratinga c. maugei*). There are very little differ-

ences between the species. Until it was hunted to extinction in the 1890s, the Mauge's were found in Puerto Rico. These conures were hunted as pests and, sadly, only the Hispaniolan can be found today. Breeding in cap-tivity has been infrequent.

Jamaican Conures

Distribution: Jamaica

Mostly green in color, Jamaican conures (*Aratinga nana*) are found in the area for which they are named. They have olive brown feathering on the throat and breast area with an olive wash further down to the abdomen. The edges of the flight feathers are dark blue, with the undersides gray, and the underside of the tail feathers are greenish yel-low. Some individuals may sport an orange feather or two around the face. The eye ring is a whitish color, and the irises are orange. The large bill is horn colored, with a gray col-oration on the base of the upper mandible as well as on the sides of the lower, and the feet are gray. Jamaican conures measure about 10 inches (25 cm) in length.

Subspecies include the Aztec conure (*Aratinga n. astec*), also known as the Olive-throated conure, and the Eastern Aztec conure (*Aratinga n. vicinalis*). In aviculture, these conures are not easy to breed and don't produce often.

Jenday Conures

Distribution: Brazil.

About 12 inches (30 cm) in size, Jenday conures (*Aratinga jandaya*)

A colorful Jenday conure.

are described as having charming, talkative personalities, and owners of these attractive conures claim that they are outgoing and acrobatic. Jendays are primarily green when viewed from the back, and they have bright yellow, orange, and red feathering in the head, face, and throat area. The abdomen, breast, and rump are orange. The flight and tail feathers are blue and green, and this conure's feet and mandibles are black. White eye rings circle the eyes, which have brown irises.

Domestic breeding of Jendays has been very successful, and hand-fed babies are usually available. Jenday conures make excellent companions, with some specimens learning to speak quite clearly. They enjoy attention and plenty of toys, and they are quite photogenic.

Mitred Conures

Distribution: Argentina, Bolivia, and Peru.

The Mitred conure (*Aratinga mitrata*) is a strikingly beautiful bird. At one time, these conures were imported by the thousands and sometimes older wild-caught birds can still be found. They don't breed well in captivity, but sometimes do produce. Their voices are loud and powerful, though singly kept birds aren't as noisy. Mitred conures can become good talkers and they make friendly, affectionate pets.

They are large birds, 15 inches (38 cm) in length, and have oversized horn-colored mandibles. Their bodies are mostly green, and they have dark red feathers on their faces, heads, napes, and throats. Some red feathers may also be found scattered on the chest and abdomen, and under the wings. The eyes are yellowish brown to tan, and the eye rings are white. They have light-colored, pinkish feet. A subspecies, the Chapman's Mitred conure (*Aratinga m. alticola*), is slightly smaller and has darker coloration, with less red feathering.

Orange-fronted Conures

Distribution: Mexico.

Orange-fronted conures (*Aratinga canicularis*) are also called Petz's conures, or half-moon conures. These little parrots were once imported from Mexico by the thousands and have been popular with bird owners for years. Since the ban on importation, those Orange-fronts that are available for sale now are mostly domestically raised. They are friendly, comical, and exhibit wonderful pet qualities.

In appearance, these conures have mostly green plumage, with orange foreheads. A ruffle of blue feathers is behind the orange patch, and the wings and tail feathers are green and blue. The eye ring is a cream color and the iris is yellow. Mandibles are horn colored, while the feet are gray. The size is usually 9.5 inches (24 cm) from head to tail. Two subspecies are very similar, with slight differences in the coloration of the orange bands, and the lower mandibles a grayish color. The *Aratinga c. eburnirostrum* and the *Aratinga c. clarae* are almost identical to the *Aratinga canicularis.*

Orange-fronted conures prefer to nest deep inside arboreal termite mounds. Duplicating this situation in captive breeding setups is difficult and the birds often don't produce. When they do, the hand-fed babies make wonderful pets.

Peach-fronted Conures

Distribution: Argentina, Bolivia, and parts of northern Paraguay.

Peach-fronted conures (*Aratinga aurea*) measure about 10 inches (25 cm) in length, and are described as being quieter than many other *Aratinga* conures. With their lower-pitched voices, these conures make good apartment pets. They love to play, learn to speak easily, are affectionate, and have bubbly personalities.

Their bodies are mostly green, with some yellowish coloration on their breasts and wing bends. They have a patch of orange on the front of the forehead that is followed by dull blue feathers extending down the back of the crown. Tail and wing feathers are predominately green, with touches of yellow and blue. The eye ring of these conures is a creamy color, and may be peach or yellow. The iris is orange, the mandibles black, and the feet are pinkish gray. The Greater Golden-crowned conure (*Aratinga a. major*) looks much the same, but is larger, at 12 inches (30 cm) in length.

In the wild, they are most often seen in pairs or in small groups, and they prefer to nest in hollowed-out branches, tree holes, arboreal termite mounds, and often in cliffs. They are not difficult to breed in captivity, and hand-fed chicks bond readily to their human companions.

A young Peach-fronted conure.

Red-fronted conure; one of the many species featuring red coloring.

Red-fronted Conures

Distribution: Colombia, Ecuador, Peru, and Venezuela.

There are many conures in this group. Each resembles the other, but some have varying amounts of red. Most are large birds, and their bright, contrasting colors make them stunning to look at.

Red-fronted conures (*Aratinga wagleri*), have large green bodies with bright red feathers on their heads and faces, and some red markings on the bends of the wings. Some birds may have red on their breast area. Their periophthalmic eye rings are white and the irises are reddish. The mandibles are large and horn colored, and the feet are gray. The birds measure about 14 inches (35.5 cm) in length, and are also called Wagler's conures.

There are several subspecies, which include the *Aratinga w. transilis,* the *Aratinga w. frontata*, and the *Aratinga w. minor*. These conures are big birds, measuring 15.5 inches (39 cm). They can be very loud at times, but are said to make excellent pets with good talking ability. Domestic breeders are working with these conures, but the birds do not often respond to the efforts, so unfortunately, they can be difficult to find.

Red-masked Conures

Distribution: Ecuador and Peru.

Red-masked conures (*Aratinga erythrogenys*) have green bodies with red faces and crowns, and red feathering under the lower mandible. The amount of red varies from individual to individual, with some birds having more red than others. White eye rings, yellow irises, and grayish feet round out their appearances. They measure 13 inches (33 cm) and have horn-colored hooked bills. They are not free breeders in aviculture, although some success has been had. Reportedly they make good talkers and can become friendly, tame pets.

St. Thomas Conures

Distribution: St. Thomas in the Virgin Islands, subspecies in Brazil, Colombia, Guyana, Panama, Venezuela, and the islands of Aruba, Margarita, and Tortuga.

Also known as Brown-throated conures, St. Thomas conures (*Aratinga pertinax*) are not commonly found in the pet market. Their main coloration is green, with an orange hue to the head and chin. There is a blue tint to the crown. There are scattered orange or red feathers about the face and neck, and the feet are gray. The mandibles are grayish to horn colored, and the eye ring is white surrounding eyes with yellow irises. These conures measure about 10 inches (25 cm) in length.

Subspecies include the *Aratinga p. xanthogenia*, the *Aratinga p. aeruginosa*, the *Aratinga p. arubensis*, the *Aratinga p. lehmanni*, the *Aratinga p. tortugensis*, the *Aratinga p. margaritensis*, *Aratinga p. venezuelae*, the *Aratinga p. chrysophrys*, and the *Aratinga p. ocularis*.

Captive breeding has occurred, but the birds are not prolific in domestic setups and babies can be difficult to find.

Sun Conures

Distribution: Brazil, French Guiana, Guyana, and Venezuela.

Often described as puppylike in their behavior, Sun conures (*Aratinga solstitialis*) are one of the most popular and beautiful conures available in the pet bird market today. Their luminous colors consist of vivid red-orange, gold, yellow, and red on the head, face, abdomen, and back. Some wing feathers are green, and flight and tail feathers are blue and green. Their smallish mandibles are black, and the feet may be varying shades of gray to black. The eye ring is white and the iris is dark brown. Young birds have more green feathers, but these baby feathers molt out

The beautiful Sun conure.

and the brilliant colors emerge as the birds mature.

About 12 inches (30 cm) in size, Sun conures are very active birds, make excellent pets, and some become good talkers. Their voices are loud and have the characteristic conure squawking tones, but they can be encouraged not to screech. Domestic breeders have had much success raising these conures, and hand-fed babies are usually available. Sun conures are extremely playful, curious, and happy to be involved in any family activities. Because of their beauty, they are

Black-capped conures (see page 21).

often used as models in magazines and advertisements.

White-eyed Conures

Distribution: Argentina, Brazil, Bolivia, Colombia, Ecuador, Guyana, Paraguay, Peru, Suriname, Uruguay, and Venezuela.

The White-eyed conure (*Aratinga l. leucophthalma*) has been described as intelligent, curious, friendly, and gentle. Its playful personality has won it many fans, and people who own White-eyed conures will argue that their birds make the best pets of all the conures.

White-eyed conures have green bodies with a few red feathers scat-tered about the head and neck area. Their green wings have red bends and red feather edges, and the tail feathers are mostly green. The irises are brown, and the periophthalmic ring is white. The feet are gray and the mandibles are horn colored. These birds reach sizes of 12.5 inches (32 cm).

Subspecies include the *Aratinga l. callogenys* and the *Aratinga l. propinqua*. They are common in their natural habitat, where they some-times associate with flocks of Blue-crowned conures. They are not prolific breeders in captivity, and few chicks are available in the pet mar-ket due to the fact that not many breeding pairs have been set up.

Conures of the Genus *Pyrrhura*

These smallest conures are quieter than the larger *Aratinga* conures, can get by with smaller cages provided that they have plenty of time outside the cage for exercise, and are as full of personality and attitude as any conure in the pet bird market. In fact, some *Pyrrhura* owners claim that their birds are the only conures they would consider keeping.

Pyrrhura conures have similar body shapes to, but are more compact than, the larger conures. And though they are small, they still need plenty of room to play and lots of interesting things to keep them occupied. Never underestimate the intelligence and boldness of these little birds!

Green-cheeked and Maroon-bellied conures are often recommended for the person who is considering "stepping up" from keeping smaller birds such as budgies and cockatiels, and are the easiest to find of the *Pyrrhura* species. Black-capped and Souance conures are becoming well known, as well.

Black-capped Conures

Distribution: Brazil, Bolivia, and Peru.

There are two subspecies of the Black-capped conure, the *Pyrrhura rupicola* and the *Pyrrhura r. sandiae*. It is thought possible that the two types are actually one species, and more research is being done to determine for certain. All Black-capped conures available in the United States are from a small pool of imported breeder stock. Babies can be difficult, but not impossible, to acquire.

Measuring just over 9 inches (23 cm) in length, these pretty birds have green backs and fronts, a band of scalloped light and dark feathering around the neck, gray-brown feathering on the forehead, an orange tint to the cheeks, a white eye ring and gray mandibles, some red on the shoulders, and light gray feet. Though noisy, they are said to make good pets but are not yet readily available in the pet trade.

Crimson-bellied Conures

Distribution: Brazil.

The Crimson-bellied Conure (*Pyrrhura p. perlata*), the Pearly Conure (*Pyrrhura p. lepida*), and the Miritiba Pearly Conure (*Pyrrhura p. coerulescens*) are all 9.5 inches (24 cm) in size and closely resemble each other in appearance. The Neumann's Pearly conure (*Pyrrhura p. anerythra*) is a bit larger. Each have green bodies, a wide band of scalloped, light-colored feathers around the neck, some blue around the chin, dark-colored crowns, bright orange-red patches on the abdomen, feathered grayish eye rings, gray feet, and dark gray upper and lower mandibles. Their unusual patterns of coloration make these conures very attractive.

Not much is known for certain about their breeding habits in the wild, but it is thought that they go to nest twice a year. In captive breeding situations, the Crimson-bellied conure has proven to be difficult to breed, though successes have been accomplished. These birds aren't normally available for pets, and owners of these conures are encouraged to set their birds up for breeding. The pool of breeder birds is limited, and too many related pairs have been used, which has resulted in problems associated with inbreeding. It is hoped that a strong stock of unrelated pairs can be established.

Fiery-shouldered Conures

Distribution: Brazil, Guyana, and Venezuela.

The 10-inch (25-cm) Fiery-shouldered conure (*Pyrrhura e. egregia*) has a green body with maroon markings on the forehead, a mostly brown head, green feathers with tan to light gray edging on the neck, throat, and chest, and a dark red patch on the abdomen. The wing

Playful Green-cheeked conures.

feathers are blue, and the tail is maroon with a green base. White eye rings surround eyes with brown irises, the mandibles are horn colored, and the feet are gray. Subspecies Gran Sabana conure (*Pyrrhura e. obscura*) closely resembles the Fiery-shouldered conure but is a darker green and measures about 9.5 inches (24 cm) in length. While information about their breeding habits in the wild is scant, these conures have been bred in captivity, though not often. Owners of these conures report that they are fairly quiet and make sweet, funny companions.

Green-cheeked Conures

Distribution: Argentina, Bolivia, and Brazil.

Green-cheeked conures (*Pyrrhura molinae*) are tiny 10-inch (25-cm) birds with huge attitudes. Small enough to nestle comfortably in a human hand, these pint-sized dynamos aren't afraid to challenge birds much larger than themselves. This fearlessness can lead to dangerous situations unless the Green-cheek owner is constantly on guard when the conure is out of its cage. Often mistaken for Maroon-bellied conures because of their similar appearances, Green-cheeks are feisty, outgoing, and sometimes nippy birds.

Green-cheeks have dark green bodies and their upper breast, throat, and nape area is covered with brownish green feathers edged with tan. They have maroon-colored abdomen patches, brownish feathers on the head, and bright green cheeks. The eye ring is white, the eyes brown, the upper and lower mandibles are gray, and the feet and legs are gray. There is also a patch of maroon coloring above the tail.

Subspecies include the Argentina conure (*Pyrrhura m. australis*), which has more maroon coloring on the abdomen, the Crimson-tailed conure (*Pyrrhura m. phoenicura*), which is a bit smaller at 9.5 inches (24 cm), the Yellow-sided conure, also called the Sordid conure (*Pyrrhura m. hypoxantha*), which can be duller in appearance with hints of blue to the cheeks, and the Santa Cruz conure (*Pyrrhura m. restricta*), which may exhibit more blue on the wings and measures about 9.5 inches (24 cm) in length.

Since these conures have been bred so successfully in captivity, hand-fed babies are usually available. They are fairly quiet, can learn to say a few words, and make wonderful, affectionate, bossy pets.

Maroon-bellied Conures

Distribution: Argentina, Bolivia, Brazil, Paraguay, and Uruguay.

The Maroon-bellied conure (*Pyrrhura f. frontalis*) is a 10-inch (25-cm) bird with handsome markings. Mostly green, it has bronze bars on the chest, green flight feathers touched with blue, and green tail feathers that have a reddish tint. There is a patch of dark red on the abdomen and lower back. This conure has a white eye ring and brown eyes, dark gray to black upper and lower mandibles, and gray legs and feet. In the wild, Maroon-bellied

Maroon belly.

conures often make pests of themselves by scavenging crops and fruit orchards. The damage they cause puts them in danger of being hunted, trapped, or killed.

Subspecies include the Azara's conure (*Pyrrhura f. chiripepe*), which is also 10 inches (25 cm) in size and closely resembles the *frontalis*, save for greener tail feathers. Some of these birds may have red feathers on their wings. The Blaze-winged conure (*Pyrrhura f. devillei*) is smaller, and looks much the same in appearance as the Azara's but has more brown coloring on the head.

Friendly by nature, these conures often preen and groom their human flock members. They are domestically bred on a regular basis, and hand-fed babies are usually available. Charming, intelligent, and playful, Maroon-bellied conures can learn to say a few words, and their vocalizations are not as piercing as some of the larger conures. They sometimes exhibit aggression toward other birds or pets, so care must be taken that they don't get themselves into trouble. Avid bathers, Maroon-bellies should always have lots of fresh, clean water at their disposal.

Maroon-tailed Conures

Distribution: Colombia, Ecuador, and Peru.

The Maroon-tailed conure (*Pyrrhura melanura*) is often called the Souance conure (*Pyrrhura melanura souancei*). These 9.5-inch (24-cm) birds are mostly green, with red on the wing edges, a scalloped band of light-colored feathers around the neck, gray mandibles, white eye rings, and dark eyes and feet. Since only small numbers of these birds were imported, they are fairly rare in aviculture. They have been successfully raised in captivity but not many babies are available yet in the pet market. They are said to make excellent companions.

Painted Conures

Distribution: Bolivia, Brazil, Guyana, Suriname, and Venezuela.

These beautiful birds are not commonly seen in aviculture, and few are available as pets. Placing these birds into breeding situations is strongly encouraged and most are sold as breeders rather than as pets. People owning these conures claim that they have wonderful pet qualities and personalities comparable to those of Green-cheeks.

Their bodies are green with red bellies and rumps, and there is some blue on the primary wing feathers.

They have scalloped light and dark feathering on the upper breast and neck, red patches under the eyes, blue on the forehead, white or light-colored ear coverts, darker feathering on the back of the head, tan or gray feet, and white eye rings. The unusual coloring of the Painted conure (*Pyrrhura picta picta*) gives it an exotic appearance.

Subspecies include the *Pyrrhura p. amazonum*, the *Pyrrhura p. microtera*, the *Pyrrhura p. lucianii*, the *Pyrrhura p. subandina*, the *Pyrrhura p. caeruleiceps*, the *Pyrrhura p. pantchenkoi*, and the *Pyrrhura p. eisenmanni*. The Rose-headed conure (*Pyrrhura p. roseifrons*) is protected by strict exportation laws. It has a brilliant red head, forehead, and nape, and is a stunningly beautiful bird.

Aviculturists are working to produce healthy babies to add to the stock of unrelated breeder birds. It is hoped that this lovely conure will soon be available to the pet market in greater numbers.

White-eared Conures

Distribution: Brazil and Venezuela.

White-eared conures (*Pyrrhura leucotis*) have green bodies, red bellies, red feathering on the shoulder, light-colored upper breast areas that appear to be scalloped, brown faces, black mandibles, dark eye rings with brown irises, and light brown feet. One of the smallest conures, they measure approximately 8.5 inches (21 cm) in length.

Subspecies include the *Pyrrhura l. griseipectus,* the *Pyrrhura l. pfrimeri,* the *Pyrrhura l. emma,* and the *Pyrrhura l. auricularis.* While some of these conures have been successfully captive bred in Europe for many years, not all of them are commonly seen in the United States. It is said that they are energetic, playful, and blend easily into their human families.

Conures of the Genus *Nandayus*

Nanday Conures

Distribution: Argentina, Brazil, Bolivia, and Paraguay.

There is only one conure in this group, and that is the Nanday conure (*Nandayus nenday*). Closely resembling the *Aratinga* genus in breeding habits, body shape, and vocalizations, Nandays are beautiful 12-inch (30-cm) birds with unusual coloring. The body is bright green, the head is black, and there is a wash of blue on the throat and upper chest. Flight feathers are blue and the tail is blue with black undersides. Bright red feathers mark the lower legs, and the feet are light colored. The eye ring is white and surrounds brown eyes. Upper and lower mandibles are black.

Nandays reproduce readily in captivity, and the hand-fed chicks make wonderful, affectionate pets. Some even develop clear vocabularies. The main drawback to keeping Nandays is their harsh, grating call, but Nandays kept as only birds can be taught to be quieter. Very intelligent, hardy,

White-eared conure.

Nanday.

acrobatic, and clownish, Nandays make great pets for the person who is prepared to deal with their noise.

Conures of the Genus *Cyanoliseus*

Patagonian Conures, Andean Conures

Distribution: Argentina, Chile, and Uruguay.

Patagonian conures are the largest conures of all. Their body shape has been compared to that of mini macaws, with some Patagonians being larger than a few species of mini macaws. The Patagonian conure (*Cyanoliseus p. patagonus*) and the Andean Patagonian (*Cyanoliseus p. andinus*) both measure 18 inches (46 cm) in size. The Greater Patagonian conure (*Cyanoliseus p. byroni*) is a bit larger, measuring 19 inches (48 cm) from head to tail tip. Their general descriptions are much the same. All birds have olive green feathering over

A pair of Pearly conures.

most of their bodies, with sparse white feathering in the neck area of some individuals. The abdomen and legs are reddish orange and there is blue on the primary wing feathers and the tail. In some individuals, especially the Andean Patagonian, the abdomen may not exhibit as much orange or red coloration, and some may have none at all. The bright white periophthalmic eye ring narrows to a point behind the eye, and the irises are yellow. Both upper and lower mandibles are black and the feet are pink.

While the Patagonian (*Cyanoliseus p. patagonus*) and the Andean Patagonian (*Cyanoliseus p. andinus*) are not considered endangered, the Greater Patagonian (*Cyanoliseus p. byroni*) is becoming rare. These birds are trapped in great numbers for trade. And not only has the number of Patagonian conures in the wild dwindled due to trapping, but because of their habit of raiding crops, they are hunted and destroyed as pest birds.

Patagonian conures bond well with their owners, often choosing a specific person as a favorite. They can learn to speak, enjoy playing rough-and-tumble games, and have very loud voices. The shriek of a Patagonian can be earsplitting. These conures have the unusual habit of sometimes diving down instead of flying upward when startled. Because of their large size, they need big cages with appropriately sized perches. They enjoy splashing around in water and spending time with their owners. Hand-fed babies make exceptional pets.

Unusual Conures

The Austral conure and the Slender-billed conure are not commonly seen in the pet trade, but are slowly becoming more well known. These conures are large birds, with pretty colorings and markings. They require the same diets as other conures, and should be housed in roomy cages appropriate to their sizes.

Conures of the Genus *Enicognathus*

Austral Conures
Distribution: Argentina.

The Austral conure (*Enicognathus f. ferrugineus*) is mostly green, with dark-edged feathers. Its forehead, lores (area over the nostrils), and abdomen are maroon. The wings are green, tinged with blue, and the tail is maroon with green tips. With dark gray to black upper and lower mandibles, dark red irises, gray skin in the eye ring, and gray feet, this bird is striking in appearance. In size, the Austral conure measures 14.5 inches (37 cm) in length. The Chilean conure (*Enicognathus f. minor*) is slightly smaller, measuring 13.5 inches (34 cm) from head to tail. It looks much like the Austral conure but is darker in color. Austral conures have been successfully bred in captivity.

Austral conure.

Slender-billed Conures
Distribution: Chile.

The main coloring of the Slender-billed conure (*Enicognathus leptorhynchus*) is green, with a dark edging to the feathers. There is an obvious maroon coloring to the forehead, lores, and abdomen. The wing feathers are green with a blue tinge, and the tail feathers are dark red. The eye ring is gray and the iris orange or red. Its feet are gray, and the mandibles are dark, with the upper part curved, narrow, and sharp. This is a big bird, measuring nearly 16 inches (41 cm) in length.

Captive breeding programs have been successful. Playful, curious, and intelligent, these conures particularly enjoy bathing.

Endangered Conures

Yellow-eared Conure

Distribution: The Andes of Colombia, and Ecuador.

The Yellow-eared conure (*Ognorhynchus icterotis*) is a mostly green bird, with yellow cheeks, ears, and lores. The lower part of the face is green, with the chest and abdomen a lighter green. Tail feathers are maroon, the eye ring is dark colored and surrounds orange eyes, the mandibles are dark gray to black, and the feet are gray. It is a large bird, measuring about 16.5 inches (42 cm) in length.

The Yellow-eared conure prefers to live in forested and mountainous areas. Already rare in its native habitat, this conure is in danger of extinction. Only a couple of hundred are estimated to still inhabit the areas. While it's not certain what has caused the decline of these conures, it is thought that deforestation and loss of natural habitat are to blame. Not much is known about their breeding habits except that they nest in colonies. These conures are only rarely kept in captivity.

Golden-Plumed Conures

Distribution: Colombia and parts of the Andes in Ecuador and Peru.

About 10 inches (25 cm) in length, Golden-plumed conures (*Leptosittaca branickii*) are mostly green with orange foreheads. Their faces have some yellow feathering and they have orange patches on their abdomens. Tail feathers are green with maroon underneath, the mandible is horn colored, the eye rings are white, and the irises are orange. The feet are gray.

Golden-plumed conures prefer the higher elevations and live in the cloud forest. Usually seen in small groups, they have been spotted in larger flocks of up to 50 birds. Active birds, they are seldom in one spot for long and spend a great deal of time moving from tree to tree.

Their diet consists of pinecone seeds, fruits, especially figs, various seeds, and grain pilfered from maize fields. Due to their habit of raiding crops, they are considered pest birds in some locations. Deforestation and loss of habitat have contributed to their decline in the wild. They are seldom kept in captivity.

The Extinct Conures of the Genus *Conuropsis*

The Carolina Parakeet, the Louisiana Parakeet

The United States was once home to two types of conures, the Carolina conure, most commonly referred to as the Carolina parakeet (*Conuropsis c. carolinensis*), which was native to the southeastern United States, and the Louisiana parakeet (*Conuropsis c. ludovicianus*), which was found in Colorado, Indiana, Kentucky, Nebraska, Ohio, Oklahoma, Tennessee, West Virginia, and Wisconsin. These birds are now extinct, due to the destruction of their natural habitats, being trapped for trade, and being killed as pests by farmers tired of finding their crops destroyed by the birds.

The Carolina parakeet was a 12-inch (30-cm) bird with yellow-green coloring over most of its body. Orange feathers covered the forehead and face, and the wing feathers were green, edged with yellow. The eye ring was white and the irises brown, while the feet were tan to brown, and the hooked bill was horn colored. The last known specimen of the Carolina parakeet died in 1918 at the Cincinnati Zoo.

The Louisiana parakeet, also 12 inches (30 cm), looked much the same, but had more blue and turquoise coloring. Until their destruction, these birds lived in wooded areas and favored locations near rivers, swamps, and other bodies of water. Orchards, gardens, fields of grain, and other agricultural areas were favorite feeding places. They would also dig up and consume bits of earth for the minerals it contained.

They were sometimes seen in large flocks of several hundred birds feeding together. Their preferred roosting places were in high tree branches. Not much is known about their breeding habits except that they nested in holes in trees.

Chapter Three

Choosing the Right Conure

Now that you've learned about the different species of conures, you are aware that each one has certain requirements, habits, and personality traits, and that these traits and requirements can vary widely among individual birds within any species. Use the information you've accumulated to help determine which conure will be the most compatible with you and your personality traits, those of your family, and with your lifestyle. The following questionnaire will be helpful as you make your decision.

Questions and Considerations

1. *Do you live in an apartment?* Some leases that don't allow dogs or cats will allow birds, but it's very important to check and see what your lease agreement says before you choose a conure. You will also want to discuss noise issues with

Jenday conures are beautiful, but can be noisy.

your landlord or next-door neighbors before bringing home a conure.

Some species of conures will be too noisy for apartment living unless the building has soundproof walls. Patagonian and Nanday conures are extremely loud, and most *Aratinga* conures have big, screechy voices and can be quite vocal at certain times of day. A few of the loudest *Aratinga* conures are Cherry-headed conures, Jenday conures, Mitred conures, and Sun conures. Keep in mind that individual birds may be quieter (or louder) than expected. It's said that the Peach-fronted conure isn't as loud as other *Aratinga* conures and so is sometimes recommended as a good apartment bird.

Pyrrhura conures have quieter voices. Even so, they can be quite noisy, especially when more than one is kept. A single *Pyrrhura* conure would make a fine apartment bird. Maroon-bellied conures and Green-cheeked conures are usually easy to find, and the hand-fed babies become wonderful, entertaining pets. Other *Pyrrhura* conures, such as the Painted conure, the Souance conure, and the White-eared conure also make good apartment birds, but can be difficult to find and are very expensive. These conures are better kept in breeding situations until larger numbers of their kind are available.

2. *Do you have room in your home for a spacious cage, accessories, and a playstand?* The larger *Aratinga* and Patagonian conures require big cages, and parrot-sized cages are recommended for them. Nandays also appreciate roomy cages. But if you are planning to allow your conure to have plenty of out-of-the-cage time for play and exercise, a smaller cage can be used for sleeping and mealtimes.

If your home is tight on space, perhaps a *Pyrrhura* conure would be a better fit. They can live comfortably in cockatiel-sized cages as long as they have lots of out-of-the-cage time for exercise. A smaller house or apartment will usually be able to accommodate a cage this size.

Whatever type of conure you decide on, plan on allowing plenty of room where the bird can play, and enough floor space for playstands and toys. Spoiled conures and their accumulated stuff can take over a house.

3. *Are you a day sleeper?* Unless you can keep your conure's cage far from your bedroom, expect to hear squawks, screeches, and yells while you are trying to sleep. By nature, conures are very vocal birds and should be allowed a certain amount of normal, happy squawk time every day.

4. *Do you have your heart set on a talking bird?* Most conures can learn to say at least their names, and a rare few develop impressive vocabularies. While their talking skills will never match those of larger parrots, their voices are amusing and fun to listen to. Hand-fed conures learn to talk more rapidly than older birds, and many hand-fed babies learn to say a few words before they are weaned.

Some conures that are known to talk are Blue-crowns, Jendays, Mitred conures, Nandays, Patagonian conures, Peach-

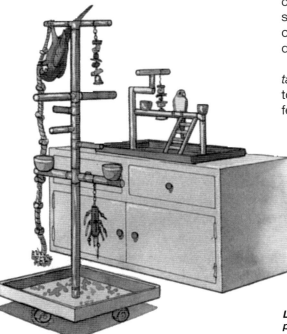

Large wheeled playstand; tabletop playgym.

A pair of Sun conures.

fronts, and Sun conures. Green-cheeks and Maroon-bellied conures can also learn a few words, but their voices may not be as understand-able as those of the larger conures. Please be aware that not all parrots, even those famous for their talking skills, such as African greys or some Amazons, will speak. It's up to the individual conure whether or not an understandable word will ever pass its beak. Are you prepared to love your conure for itself and not to be disappointed if it never says a word?

5. *Are there already other pets in the household?* If so, be prepared for a bit of jealousy when the new conure comes home. You might want to bring a special treat to the dog or cat to help soothe hurt feelings. And always, always, *always* supervise any interactions between your conure and other pets or birds. Some conures, especially Green-cheeks and Maroon-bellies, are so indepen-dent and bossy that they won't hesi-tate to challenge a larger pet.

6. *Do you already have a bird at home?* If so, it is vitally important to quarantine your new conure in a room away from the existing bird. A general recommended quarantine time is usually 30 to 45 days, but consult your avian veterinarian to be certain that will be sufficient. Always make sure to have a new conure

A Green-cheeked conure and friend.

cases, conures enjoy the attention of children and quickly become friends with them. Many conures learn to say the names of children in the household, and usually hand-fed conures adapt better to children than do adult birds. Be prepared to supervise all interactions until you are certain the child understands that the conure is not a toy and can be hurt by rough handling.

8. *What's your personality type?* Someone who is high-strung or nervous probably wouldn't be happy with one of the larger, noisier conures such as Nandays or Patagonians. While they are beautiful birds, their loud voices and boisterous personalities will soon cause them to wear out their welcomes. A few *Aratinga* conures that are calm and easy to handle are Blue-crowns, Peach-fronts, and Orange-fronts. Again, much depends on the individual personality of the conure. *Pyrrhura* conures such as Maroon-bellies and Green-cheeks can be good choices, but there are huge personalities packed inside those tiny bodies. Unless you're prepared to deal with a headstrong little featherhead that thinks it's the boss, select a more sedate conure. Ask a breeder or other experienced conure keeper for recommendations.

If you are relaxed and easygoing, you'll probably enjoy just about any type of conure. Conures are always ready to play, and many will clown around just to make their human companions laugh. It's not unusual to see them hanging by one toe

evaluated by a qualified avian veterinarian to rule out any health issues before you take it home to be with your other birds. Sometimes, conures can be silent carriers of diseases that may not affect them but can kill other birds after exposure. The same can be said of other species of parrots, too.

7. *Are there children in the home?* Conures and children can successfully mix, providing that certain things are kept in mind. Some conures can be nervous around children, especially very young children. To avoid nipping or biting, teach children not to tease your conure and not to poke their fingers into the cage. In some from the top of the cage, beating up their toys, or rolling around in the bottom of the cage on their backs. They love singing along with the radio and dancing, taking baths, tearing up magazines and junk mail, and yelling along with the noises from broadcast sporting events or loud television programs. Conures are extremely interactive pets.

9. *Are you sensitive to noise?* If so, a single *Pyrrhura* conure may be the best choice for you. Their voices aren't as powerful as the *Aratinga*, Nanday, or Patagonian conures, but they can still produce a lot of noise. To cut down on excessive screeching, offer fun, chewable toys, lots of attention, plenty of baths, and adequate playtime outside of the cage.

10. *Does messiness bother you?* If so, here's the bad news: Conures love to shred their tray liners, throw food out of the cage, drop toys, and generally make as many messes as they can. You'll have to be prepared to do extra housekeeping if you bring a conure into your home. The good news is that conures are so much fun, you probably won't mind! But before you can choose a conure, you must be able to find a conure.

Shopping for a Conure

While pet stores and bird stores are likely places to start, you may also be able to find healthy conures by looking for conure breeders on-line or in avian publications, by scan-ning the want ad section of your local newspaper, or by asking for refer-ences at veterinary clinics. You may even know someone who breeds conures. Don't be shy when it comes to learning about the conures you find. Ask all the questions you need! This is an important decision, both for you and for your conure.

Pet Stores and Bird Stores

Just because a store sells conures doesn't mean that it's a good place to choose your new companion. Here are a few things you should keep in mind before you step through the door:
• A good store will be clean and well lit, and stocked with a variety of quality foods, accessories, and cages.
• Employees and managers should be knowledgeable about conures and be willing to answer your questions.
• The bird area should be tidy, adequately heated or cooled, and the cages clean.
• Food and water cups in the bird cages should be clean and filled.
• Litter or cage liners should be both odor- and insect-free, with no big piles of droppings under the perches.
• The birds shouldn't be crowded into the cages, and under no circumstances should you ever see a dead or obviously sick bird!
• Any open play areas should be monitored.
• Baby birds should be in safe, temperature-controlled enclosures.

Carefully observe the store's selection of conures and ask yourself these questions:

1. Are all the conures playing and vocalizing, healthy and energetic?

2. Are the ones that appear to be napping really just sleeping and not sick?

3. Do the workers comfortably interact with the conures and seem enthusiastic about them?

4. Are they willing to chat with you and answer any questions?

5. Does the store offer a health guarantee? A good minimum time span is from 48 to 72 hours so that you can have the conure you're interested in checked by an avian veterinarian.

A store that fits this description would probably be a safe place to purchase a bird of any type. Steer clear of stores that smell of urine or feces, have sick animals on display, or are too dimly lit to allow for safety. Birds shouldn't be crowded into cages that are too small with bars and perches that are covered with droppings, and there should never be sick birds mixed in with the healthy ones. Run, don't walk, away from a store like this as fast as you can! Never purchase a conure that has been kept in such an environment. While you may get lucky and find a healthy conure, chances are great that any type of animal purchased from such an establishment would have problems.

Conure Breeders

Breeders should be checked out as carefully as pet stores. Breeding facilities can be big operations with lots of different types of birds, or the facility might be a single room in someone's home. Don't be put off if the breeder you find has a small setup in his or her house. As long as strict sanitary conditions are maintained, the breeder is qualified to raise conures, the breeder birds and chicks are well fed and all their requirements met, baby conures from these situations should be as healthy as those from other breeding operations.

If you do find a breeder who will let you visit the facilities, drop by to look around and take note of the general environment. If the breeder birds and young are kept in dark, dirty surroundings, are crowded into cages that are too small, if the area smells bad, or if there are caked-up piles of feces in the bottoms of the cages, walk away. Not only is there the chance that a conure bred under these conditions will have health problems, but to purchase from someone who has such little regard for the birds will be to encourage further bad treatment. Look for a facility that is well lit, clean, smells fresh, has cages set up to provide plenty of room for each pair of breeder conures, and enough clean, sanitary enclosures for the babies.

Understand that very few breeders will allow customers into the adult bird breeding area due to concerns about disease transmission, fears of upsetting the birds, of interfering with the routine, or other disruptions. The baby bird area will most likely be open to inspection provided a few basic rules of disinfection are followed.

The breeder you choose should be well educated about conures and willing to answer any questions you have. Don't be surprised if you aren't allowed to see or handle the baby birds. Many breeders won't let someone from outside the facility touch the chicks, or even visit the nursery. Don't be offended if this happens. This is a good thing. It means that the breeder takes the safety of the conures seriously.

Sometimes a breeder may let you handle a baby conure if you agree to wash your hands first, and some may even ask you to put on surgical scrubs before going into the nursery. Don't be surprised by requests like these—everything is being done for the welfare of the breeding conures and their chicks.

Advertisements

Sometimes conures can be found by searching newspaper ads. These birds may be offered at a great price, and might even come with a cage and accessories. But before you rush to spend your money on a conure like this, check out every detail. Make a list of questions, and don't be afraid to *ask* them. You might start with a few questions like these:
• Does the conure have health problems?
• Is it fully weaned?
• How old is it?
• Does it have behavioral problems, such as biting, excessive screaming, or feather picking?
• Is the seller the original owner, after the breeder or pet store? If not,

Whether selling canaries or conures, knowledgeable store personnel should be able to answer any of your questions.

does the seller have any history on the conure?

That great deal may not be so great if the conure is sick, or is so obnoxious that no one can live with it. But not all conures sold through advertisements are bad business. Sometimes wonderful conures can be bought from people who are moving, changing jobs, having a baby, going through a divorce, or experiencing some other life change that won't allow for a busy, noisy conure. If you come across an ad for a conure that sounds just right for you, make sure to see it in person before you decide to buy it. It might turn out to be the deal of a lifetime.

Choosing a Baby Conure

A hand-fed baby conure will be tamed and sweet when you adopt it. Occasionally some babies need to be encouraged to bond with their new owners, but for the most part a hand-fed bird is ready to become your best friend.

How to Distinguish Between a Healthy Baby Conure and a Sick Baby Conure

There are certain things to look for when choosing a healthy baby conure. The baby should have bright eyes and be active, alert, and vocal. It should be fully feathered, plump, and well fed. Its nostrils should be clear, and the feathers around the vent (the area from which the feces come out) should be clean.

Sometimes, a baby that is still being hand-fed will have dried formula stuck to its face. This shouldn't be mistaken for spitting up or vomiting. If the baby conure you're interested in has "stuff" crusted on its head feathers, ask the breeder or retailer to make sure what's going on.

Here are some things to avoid when looking for a baby conure:

Baby Sun conures in the nest box.

These healthy baby Gold-caps look somewhat like little porcupines!

Healthy baby Green-cheeks.

• Chicks that are weak, too quiet, or too aggressive
• Babies that have matted, stained, or sticky vent feathers
• Babies that are sneezing, wheezing, or having other breathing difficulties
• Chicks that are extremely timid or shy
• Skinny babies that have thin feathering or bare patches

You'll also want to make sure that the baby's beak is not misshapen, and that its feet and legs are not twisted or deformed. However, don't be shocked if healthy baby conures look somewhat ragged. Until the first molt, most very young conures will have rough-looking feathers. Baby conures love to tumble around and wrestle with each other, they break feathers, and they sometimes chew on the feathers of their siblings. Their pinfeathers will be sticking out every

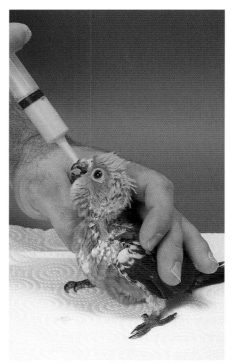

Young Sun conure being hand-fed.

which way and they might look like little porcupines! But don't worry. After the first molt, the chick that was once very bedraggled and homely will turn into a beautifully feathered conure.

Important: Before you purchase any baby conure, ask that it be veterinarian-checked and cleared of any health problems.

Choosing an Older Conure

Sometimes, mature conures, breeder conures, or formerly owned conures are offered for sale. These conures can have wonderful pet potential when given a chance.

Follow the same guidelines when looking at an older bird as you would when searching for a baby:
• The conure's eyes should be clear and bright, and the nostrils dry and not clogged.
• The head and face feathers should be clean, glossy, and not matted up, which could signify that the conure has been sneezing or vomiting.
• The vent area should be clean and not stained, and the conure should be at a healthy weight and not skinny or bony.
• Look at the conure's chest to see if the keel bone (the curved bone in the front of the chest) is prominent. It shouldn't stick out too far, which could indicate that the conure is too thin. Neither should it be encased in fat. The area should be muscular and firm.

• Listen to the conure's breathing. It shouldn't wheeze or rattle, and when it's sitting on the perch its tail shouldn't bob up and down when it breathes. If you notice any of these things, suspect a respiratory problem. Also, there should be no swelling around the eyes, and no nasal discharge. These could be symptoms of a sinus infection.
• The conure should have an alert, active personality, and should also be vocal. A conure that is extremely shy or too quiet may be ill.
• Carefully study the feathering and make sure there are no signs that

Flint, the Patagonian Conure

Flint, a mature female Patagonian conure, was adopted by a new family after spending several years in another home. She was very vocal, very loud, and extremely outgoing. While she liked everyone in the family, she almost immediately bonded with the adult male of the household. Flint was devoted to him, and spent hours on his shoulder, grooming his hair, eyebrows, and mustache, vocalizing softly the whole time. One day she snuggled against his neck, crooned in his ear, and laid an egg! Imagine the man's shock when the warm, white egg rolled down his chest and landed in his lap. Flint was a wonderful example of how adaptable some mature adult conures can be.

the bird has plucked or chewed any feathers, and that there are no bald or thin spots. All feathers should be shiny, clean, and well groomed. If the conure is molting, expect it to look a bit ragged. Just make sure that it is only molting, and not dropping feathers for any other reason. You'll want an avian veterinarian to examine the conure and give it a clean bill of health before you buy it.

• You'll also want to find out why the conure is being sold. As long as the conure is sound and in good health, has an agreeable personality, and suits you, don't hesitate to buy it. Many secondhand conures make excellent pets. But be wary of making "sympathy purchases"—if the conure is sick or has behavioral issues, it can be more trouble than it is worth.

Boy or Girl?

Conures of either sex make wonderful pets. And since you can't really tell the boys from the girls by looking, there are tests that will determine this for you. One reliable, commonly used test requires that one of the conure's toenails be clipped short enough to cause bleeding. A drop of blood is then collected and tested. Another method is done on DNA obtained from a plucked feather. The DNA material is then sent to a laboratory for tests. If you are interested in finding out the sex of your conure, ask your avian veterinarian for more details.

Of course, unless you are planning to breed your conure, this really isn't necessary. Some conure keepers say that male conures are more high-strung and a bit nippier, while some say the same thing about female conures. The truth is that each conure has its own distinct personality, and its temperament will depend on that.

Leg Bands

Your conure will more than likely have a band on one leg. Depending on the conure you're looking at, the band will either be an import band or a breeder's band.

Import bands, or open bands, are found on older conures that were brought into the country before 1992 when importation was still common. These bands were placed on legally imported parrots and identified them as having gone through the recommended period of quarantine.

Import bands

Import bands are easy to recognize. They are made of rounded metal with a gap in it. The band will be engraved with a series of letters, followed by a series of numbers. The first letter signifies the state where the quarantine station was located, the second letter is the station's code, and the third letter is part of a particular bird's I.D. number. If someone tries to sell you a "baby" conure that is wearing an open metal band, be warned—the conure is more than likely an older imported bird.

Breeder Bands

Breeder bands, or closed bands, are placed on domestically bred conures. A breeder band will be engraved with a series of letters and numbers that are the breeder's code. Letters on these bands can be traceable, or may be private codes used by some breeders.

The breeder band is a circle of metal or other material that is slid over the baby bird's foot and has no opening. Breeder bands are flat, as opposed to the rounded shape of import bands. The only unbanded baby conures you should find will probably belong to someone who privately raises a few chicks from his or her pet birds. To be on the safe side, look for a young conure that is properly banded, unless you know and trust the source.

Note: Some conure keepers remove the leg bands from their birds because they fear the bands may get caught on something and cause an injury to their conure. If you decide to remove your conure's leg band, speak with your breeder or avian veterinarian. They will record your conure's band information and keep it on file.

This Brown-throated conure is wearing a flat breeder band.

Microchips

Instead of using leg bands for identification, some breeders and hobbyists choose to have microchips implanted in their conures. The procedure involves injecting a tiny computer chip near the conure's wing. Sealed inside a grain of rice-sized glass bead, the chip is encoded with information that can be read by a special scanning device. Even the smallest conure can be microchipped in your veterinarian's office, or by the breeder. Microchips are new alternatives to leg bands that can sometimes get caught in toys or cages, and are too easily removed to provide permanent identifications. If you are interested in microchips, discuss the option with your avian veterinarian.

Choosing an Avian Veterinarian

You may be wondering what differentiates a "regular" veterinarian from an avian veterinarian. Veterinarians routinely work with dogs and cats, horses, and other animals, but with few birds. Avian veterinarians specialize in birds, and perform a wide range of services. Not only do they treat sick birds, but they do such things as clip wings, trim toenails, and perform well-bird checkups. A good avian veterinarian will be educated in the specific dietary needs of conures, will be willing to answer any questions that you may have about your conure, and will have a comfortable manner that reassures both of you. Some avian veterinarians have after-hour and weekend emergency numbers, but many do not. Try to find one who does. If your conure is going to need emergency care, you can bet that it will happen when the office is closed!

When looking for an avian veterinarian, you might ask at bird clubs, pet stores, or breeding facilities for the names and numbers of qualified specialists. Get references from people who use avian veterinarians, and then make a point to check them out. Scan the phone book for listings, and look over the ads in the backs of bird magazines. Other veterinarians are good sources; ask for recommendations. You can also check with the Association of Avian Veterinarians to find out who is available in your area. For information, visit their web site at *http://www.aav.org/aav*

Once you have located an avian veterinarian, visit the office for a question-and-answer session. You might want to include the following questions in your list:

1. How long has the doctor been treating birds?

2. Is the doctor qualified to perform surgery on your conure, if necessary?

3. Is the doctor willing to let you go into the exam room with your conure?

4. Is everything in the facility clean, tidy, and fresh smelling?

5. Is the veterinarian's staff knowledgeable, friendly, and relaxed toward birds?

6. Do they understand how to safely and comfortably handle nervous conures?

7. Are there up-to-date bird magazines, books, or other avian literature in the waiting room?

8. Do any of the staff or the veterinarian have birds of their own?

9. If the veterinarian is not available for weekend or nighttime emergencies, who do they refer these cases to?

Finally, if you can't locate a veterinarian who specializes in avian medicine, at least find one who is interested in your conure and is willing to accept it as a patient, if necessary. Don't wait until you have an emergency to start searching.

An avian scale.

should be able to return it to the store or breeder and choose another bird. If any diseases are detected, treatments can be started, and you will again have the option of keeping the conure or returning it. Preexisting health problems can be pointed out, and the age of an older conure can be estimated. Don't skip having an avian veterinarian perform an examination on the conure you are considering. It can save money and heartache in the long run.

The Trip Home

Before you head home with your brand-new conure, be sure to make proper travel arrangements. Never put a bird of any species in the trunk of a car! The exhaust fumes and unstable temperatures would kill it. Always have your conure ride in the passenger compartment, but don't let it ride loose in the vehicle, because the distraction could cause you to have an accident. The conure could be injured, too. Make sure it is contained in a sturdy travel cage or in a box appropriate to its size that it can't chew its way out of.

Special carriers designed for transporting birds are available at many stores, and you will want to either buy one of these before you take your conure home, or bring a sturdy small cage with you. Either way, don't expect to walk out of the store with your conure riding on your shoulder!

If you plan to use a cage for transport, use a small cage so that

The First Veterinary Exam

Once you've chosen a conure, you will want to have an experienced avian veterinarian examine it. The doctor will perform various tests that will include bloodwork and cultures, and will also listen to the conure's heart and chest, check its eyes and nostrils, and look inside its beak. The veterinarian should perform tests for diseases and record the conure's weight. If you have chosen a very young conure, the veterinarian will weigh the baby and tell you if it is at the correct weight for its age.

This examination is important for several reasons. If the conure you have selected has health issues, you the conure can't flap around too much and hurt itself. You might want to also bring along a towel or blanket to use for covering the cage. This will help to keep the conure from being frightened by traffic.

Note: Whether you have to cover the cage or not will depend on the individual conure, as some conures feel more secure if they can see out. And be aware that some conures get carsick. If this is the case, covering the cage or carrier might help.

Make sure to have your conure's permanent cage set up and ready at home so that you can introduce it to its new location with as little added stress as possible.

The First Few Days at Home

It's normal for a conure to be nervous or frightened in a strange, new place. It might scream, lose its appetite, or refuse to allow anyone to touch it, and you may notice watery droppings in the bottom of the cage.

• Offer lots of fresh, cool water, some of the same familiar foods the conure ate in its last home, and a few nonthreatening toys.

• Speak calmly and soothingly to your new conure, and don't make rushed or abrupt moves that will startle or confuse it.

Never try to force it to accept your attention.

• Ask that visitors and other family members also respect the conure's space. Too many strangers crowding around staring into the cage can be upsetting to an already uneasy conure.

• Keep other family pets at a distance until the conure has settled in and begun to feel safe. After a few days it should be getting used to regular household activities and can be carefully introduced to the family dog or cat. To avoid accidents, never allow other animals to have access to your conure without your constant supervision. Some pets may try to attack a newcomer, and could injure or kill an unfamiliar conure.

• If you already have other pet birds in the household, don't forget to quarantine your new conure in a separate room. Keep the doors between the rooms closed, and don't allow the birds to have contact until the recommended quarantine time is up. Change clothing and thoroughly wash your hands between handling the birds to avoid passing bacteria or viruses. Your avian veterinarian will tell you how long to continue the quarantine period. Before you know it, your new family member will settle into things and in typical conure manner try to rule the roost.

Chapter Four
Feeding Your Conure

Poor diet is a major cause of illness in caged birds, and many of the sick birds treated each year by avian veterinarians are ill as a direct result of being fed inadequate diets. Diets lacking in essential vitamins and minerals can cause problems such as poor feather condition, chronic upper respiratory infections, egg binding and calcium deficiencies in female birds, feather picking, skin problems, liver and bone disease, abnormal bleeding, and other serious conditions. Some birds even die. The good news is that you can head off potential problems by feeding your conure a well-balanced, nutritious diet.

A healthy combination for conures contains the vitamins, minerals, proteins, carbohydrates, and small amounts of monounsaturated fats that are essential for excellent avian nutrition. By providing a well-rounded diet that includes quality processed foods such as pellets or extruded foods, small amounts of an enriched seed mixture, and daily

This Gold-capped conure is enjoying a healthy snack.

servings of fresh fruits and vegetables, you can make sure your conure gets everything it needs. For the best results, see to it that 70–80 percent of its daily intake (the food it actually eats) consists of formulated diets. You can even share tiny bits of your own meals with your bird, and always be sure to provide lots of fresh, clean drinking water. Your veterinarian will be happy to help you develop a healthy feeding plan for your conure.

Conures in the Wild

Wild conures spend hours each day actively foraging for food, often traveling many miles in search of food sources. In their native habitats, conures eat berries, bugs, insect larvae, seeds, fruits, nuts, different types of vegetation, and whatever they can scavenge from agricultural areas. They are frequently seen feeding in mineral-rich soil and clay areas, and they also sometimes eat sand or bits of rock, which aid in the digestion of food. Wild conures rarely suffer from mineral deficiencies, and because they burn so many calories searching for food, they don't become overweight.

Problems with Obesity

Pet conures don't have to forage for their food, and many spend a lot of time confined to their cages. Because they aren't as active as wild conures, they often take in more calories than they can burn off, so it's not surprising that problems with obesity sometimes develop.

A chubby conure may be cute, but there are serious health risks associated with obesity and conures can experience some of the same problems humans can. Arthritis, heart disease, liver disease, diabetes, and an increased chance of developing cancer are among some of the common problems related to obesity in conures. Overweight conures also are more susceptible to infections and stress-related complications. To protect your conure from weight problems, offer it a well-balanced diet that is low in fat and oils, and plan for plenty of exercise time.

What's on the Menu?

Once upon a time, standard fare for caged birds was a bowl of seeds and a cup of water. We now know that this diet lacked essential minerals, vitamins, proteins, and other building blocks necessary for good avian health. Thanks to extensive research by nutritionists, the foods now available for pet birds are healthier and more nutritionally complete. By understanding what makes up a good avian meal plan, you will be able to offer your conure the most nutritious diet possible.

Plan to feed your conure a couple of times a day. You might offer a bowl of pellets or extruded foods for breakfast, and another serving along with some fresh vegetables for dinner. Chunks of fresh fruits make wonderful treats, or you might offer one of the yummy prepackaged types of treats sometime during the day. All of these foods, along with a small cup of a healthy seed mix from time to time, will give your conure plenty of great items from which to choose. Choices are important; after all, you'd get bored with the same old thing on your dinner plate three times a day, wouldn't you? Give your conure a variety of healthy foods and see how it pays off in shiny, healthy feathers, bright eyes, and a playful attitude.

Pellets and Extruded Foods

Pelleted diets and extruded bird foods are formulated to contain the necessary amounts of vitamins and minerals required by companion birds. Highly recommended by many veterinarians as nutritionally complete, processed foods are colorful and some come in fun, crunchy shapes. A conure that is fed a processed diet will have no need for additional dietary supplements such as vitamins. You'll find lots of processed foods to choose from in your favorite pet store, and you can even order them from mail order supply companies or off the Internet.

The differences in pellets and extruded foods can be confusing when you're first considering them. One easy way to differentiate between the foods is by looking at them. Pellets are cylindrically shaped, with rough ends where they're broken off, and are usually brown or tan in color. They are formed by the process of compression, and contain many of the same highly nutritious ingredients as extruded foods. For an added treat, fresh fruits and vegetables are cooked into some brands of pellets, and some manufacturers even add molasses to provide a tasty flavor. Each pellet is fortified with amino acids, minerals, and vitamins, and each bite contains the same amount of nutrients.

Extruded foods for pets have been around for a long time. Crunchy dry foods for cats and dogs were developed in the 1950s, and extruded foods for humans have also been around for a long time. A few familiar examples are snack foods such as corn chips and cheese curls. Extruded foods for birds came along sometime in the 1960s, when zookeepers needed a diet that would provide essential nutrients for imported birds. After much research

Conures thrive on a varied diet.

and experimentation, successful extruded foods were developed and the imports thrived on them. Before long, these foods were made available for companion birds.

What makes extruded bird foods so special? The base is formed by combining prime ingredients such as select grains, seeds, nuts, fruits, and vegetables with dietary supplements such as vitamins, proteins, and minerals. The mixture is then processed, steamed, and cooked at extremely high temperatures. Any harmful bacterium that may have been present in the ingredients are destroyed. The result is a clean, pasteurized food that smells and tastes appetizing to conures, and is visually interesting and colorful. They come in different colors and shapes, and many have appealing scents. And because vitamins,

Seed Moths

Sometimes you might find tiny moths fluttering from a container of seeds. These are seed moths and, while harmless, they can become pests. If you see webbing, empty seed hulls, or insects in your conure's seeds, you can either dispose of the whole package and buy fresh, or you can put the seeds in the freezer. This will kill the insects but won't harm the seeds. To make sure you don't end up with bugs in new seeds, never mix old seeds in with new ones.

proteins, and minerals are already in extruded foods, no additional supplements are needed.

But that doesn't mean that all dietary supplements should be omitted. Fresh vegetables and fruits should be offered daily, not just to add nutrients, but to add a fun variety to your conure's daily routine. Because extruded foods sometimes increase thirst, always make sure

Processed foods such as pellets and extruded diets are tasty and nutritious.

there is plenty of fresh, clean water in the cage at all times.

Tip: Some brightly colored extruded foods can temporarily discolor droppings.

Seed Diets

The big bags of wild birdseed you see at the grocery store may be wonderful for outside birds, but they don't come close to furnishing a well-balanced diet for companion conures. A constant diet of this type of seed mix could shorten the life expectancy of any pet bird. Full of oily sunflower seeds, wild birdseed mixes are fattening as well as deficient in amino acid and lysine, which is essential for the formation of healthy, shiny feathers. Be wary also of the cheaper pet bird mixes that contain lots of filler and cereals.

Because some stubborn conures will eat sunflower seeds to the exclusion of anything else, take care not to let that unhealthy habit get started by limiting the amounts of sunflower offered. Many healthful, prepackaged seed mixes have been developed for caged birds that are suitable for conures. Look for one that includes a wide variety of seeds and is light on nuts and sunflower seeds.

A premium seed mixture will have a broad combination of ingredients. Millet, oats and groats, various grains, Niger, safflower, pumpkin seeds, corn, canary grass seed, dried hot peppers, small amounts of sunflower seeds, and whole or shelled peanuts are some of the most common ingredients. Dried

Tips for Conversion

Some conures that have been fed a seed-only diet may not recognize pellets or extruded diets as food when first offered, and have to be trained to eat them. Because an all-seed diet is so deficient in nutrients, changing to a well-balanced diet consisting of processed foods, small amounts of healthful seeds, and fresh fruits and vegetables is a wise idea. Should you decide to switch your conure from a seed-only diet to one that includes processed foods, there are things you can do to help make the transition smoother.

• Mix the processed foods with some of your conure's favorite seeds or soft foods. Over a period of days, gradually increase the amount of pellets or extruded foods while decreasing the amount of seeds.

• You might also try moistening the pellets or extruded foods with warm water or juice, making sure to remove any uneaten wet foods after an hour or so.

• Carefully monitor the activity around the food cup to make sure that your conure is actually eating the new foods, and not just crunching them up or playing with them.

• Many finicky conures will try a new food only if they see their human companions eating it first. Make a show of tasting a bite and telling your bird how yummy it is. It may take several attempts to convince your conure to give it a try. Keep in mind that a few weeks or possibly even longer may be necessary to convert a seed-loving conure to pellets.

Once you begin making the switch from a seed mixture to a pelleted or extruded diet, give your conure plenty of time to adjust to its new food. Never take away the seeds until you are sure your bird is eating the processed foods—and never starve your conure! It's also a good idea to monitor your conure's weight during this time to make sure that the bird is actually eating. Weight loss would signify that your conure isn't eating as much as it should. Your veterinarian can offer more helpful ideas for making the conversion successful.

fruits and vegetables, as well as pellets or extruded nuggets, are also included in some brands. Some even have a delicious fruity smell! Check the package label to make sure the nutritional analysis of the diet you choose has a balanced amount of vitamins, proteins, minerals, fiber, fats, and amino acids.

Tip: Save whatever seeds your conure doesn't eat and pour them into a clean container to share with the wild birds.

Sprouted Seeds

Many people enjoy fresh sprouts in salads, but did you know that they are good for your conure, too?

Sprouts

Always rinse sprouts carefully before feeding them to your conure, never use old sprouts, and be sure to throw away any that smell bad or look moldy. While they can be a wonderful food, sprouts also can be breeding grounds for dangerous bacteria, so use special caution if you wish to feed them to your conure.

Fresh seed sprouts contain vitamins, minerals, enzymes, and proteins. A good source of vitamins A, B, and E, sprouts also contain calcium, potassium, and magnesium, along with several trace minerals. And instead of buying them, you can sprout seeds at home. A few seeds that are easy to work with are alfalfa, buckwheat, chickpeas, lentils, and sunflower. Experiment with various seeds to see what your conure likes best.

There are several ways to sprout seeds. One easy way is to fill a large jar, shallow bowl, or tray with water and add a handful of seeds; be careful not to crowd too many into your container. Then soak the seeds overnight. The next morning, drain the seeds in a colander. Rinse them with cool water a few times a day, drain, and allow fresh air to circulate around the seeds. Be sure to place the soaked seeds where they will receive indirect sunlight, and you will soon be rewarded with tiny green shoots.

You can also grow sprouts in flats of soil, either indoors or depending on the time of year, outside. Plant a layer of birdseed in shallow, well-drained soil, and then water. Be careful not to let your seed garden get too dry, and make sure to keep the area clean. Soon you'll see tiny sprouts breaking through the surface. When they reach the size you desire, pick them, rinse, and serve them. Most conures relish the tender shoots, and you may even enjoy some of them yourself!

A healthful combination of seeds and nuts.

People Food

Sit down to dinner with your conure on your shoulder and see what happens. It won't take long for you to discover that conures love people food! As long as greasy, sugary, and salty foods are avoided, many of the dishes that you make for yourself are healthy and tasty for conures. If you and your family eat low-fat, nutritious foods, you can feel free to share meals with your conure. Just remember never to let it take food from your mouth because the bacteria in human saliva can make birds sick. Here are some things to consider when setting a place at the table for your conure:

• Most conures enjoy an occasional snack of peanut butter. A bit of low-fat peanut butter on an unsalted cracker or an apple chunk will be relished, as will peanut butter mixed with raisins. However, you should be careful not to serve peanut butter too often because of the fat content.

• Some other foods enjoyed by conures are pasta, scrambled eggs, toast, rice, unbuttered pancakes with no syrup, mashed potatoes, macaroni and cheese, oatmeal, grits, cornbread, unbuttered and unsalted popcorn, unsalted crackers, spaghetti and plain sauce, and occasional tastes of ice cream. Go easy on the dairy products, because avian systems aren't designed to process them. Pizza is another conure favorite.

• Conures also readily devour chopped hard-boiled eggs and the shells (boiled for at least ten to fifteen minutes to kill any possible bacteria), very well-done chicken or turkey and the cracked bones, tuna packed in water and well drained, and cottage cheese. If you wish to give these items to your conure, offer low-fat types of cheese, and only the leanest, well-cooked meats.

• Most conures enjoy warm food, and for some hand-fed conures, warm foods are comfort foods. If you are using a microwave oven, make sure that the food has cooled

It's fun to share food with your conure; just don't let it take food out of your mouth.

down and that there are no hot spots in it before you give it to your conure. Because microwave ovens sometimes heat food unevenly, always test anything first by sticking your finger into the center of the serving. If it's too hot for you, it's too hot for your conure. Food that is too hot could result in severe crop burns or painful burnt tongues.

Fresh Vegetables

Many vegetables, especially dark green leafy ones, are good sources of vitamin A and beta carotene. Vitamin A is necessary for healthy skin and feather condition, and helps maintain a strong immune system and good eyesight. It also helps protect the mucous membranes of the throat, mouth, lungs, and gastrointestinal tract.

A variety of fresh vegetables.

Vegetables can be served either raw, cooked, or lightly steamed. Overcooking destroys some of the vitamin content so be careful not to cook vegetables too long. Don't add any fat or butter to vegetables prepared for your conure, and don't serve a lot of canned vegetables. Much of the nutritional value is destroyed during the canning process, and they can be very high in sodium. Frozen vegetables are a good choice and are easy to serve. Thaw them in warm water or heat them in a microwave, always being sure to check for hot spots before handing them over to your conure.

Some stubborn conures may refuse to try vegetables. To tempt a picky eater, offer fresh vegetables cut up into bite-sized pieces, or coarsely chop them. You might also try weaving leafy greens through cage bars. Grate hard vegetables such as carrots and yams, or cut them into interesting shapes. Get creative and use a potato peeler to carve vegetables into strings. If you make the vegetables into toys, your conure won't be able to resist picking and poking at them.

Note: Some strongly colored vegetables, such as beets, can make your conure's droppings look bloody or very dark!

Vegetables rich in vitamin A include:
- Asparagus
- Beets
- Broccoli
- Brussels sprouts
- Carrots
- Collard greens
- Dark leafy romaine lettuce
- Hot chili peppers
- Mustard greens
- Sweet potatoes
- Turnip greens
- Winter squash
- Yams

While not all vegetables contain high amounts of vitamin A, many are enjoyed by conures and can be offered regularly. Fresh corn on the cob, zucchini, cauliflower, green beans, peas, and cucumber are a few other vegetables that are tasty and attractive to conures. Because it is mostly water and contains few nutrients, don't feed your conure iceberg lettuce.

Fresh Fruits

High in water content and fiber, most fruits don't contain as many vitamins and minerals as fresh vegetables, but are rich in vitamin C. Vitamin

C is helpful because it can help ward off some types of bleeding disorders or other health problems.

Wild conures frequently eat an assortment of berries, mangos, coconut, melons, and certain citrus fruits, and few pet conures will turn their beaks up at fruit. In fact, most will insist on sharing whatever fruits their human companions are enjoying. Because some fruits cause watery droppings, don't be alarmed if your conure's droppings look different after eating a juicy piece of fruit. Some items, such as pomegranates, can also make the droppings look bloody!

A few fruits irresistible to conures are:
• Apples
• Bananas
• Blueberries
• Cantaloupe
• Figs
• Grapes
• Kiwi
• Mango
• Nectarines
• Papaya
• Peaches
• Pineapple
• Pomegranates
• Raisins
• Strawberries
• Watermelon

Wash any fresh fruit well, then cut into chunks or slices, and serve. It's not necessary to peel the fruit, but you might want to remove the seeds first. Those little single-serving-sized boxes of raisins make great fruit treats for conures. To add to the fun, not only does the conure get to shred the box, there's a tasty snack waiting inside!

Dangerous Food Items

Some foods intended for humans are deadly to conures and should be kept strictly off limits. If you plan to serve any of these items, make sure everyone in the house knows not to share with the conure!

• Chocolate is toxic to animals, and especially to birds. It contains a compound called theobromine, and conures, with their small sizes and rapid metabolisms, are extremely sensitive to its effects. Chocolate toxicity is signified by vomiting, diarrhea, seizures, heart arrhythmias, hyperactivity, unusually dark droppings, and sometimes death. If you think your conure has gotten hold of

Conures love fresh fruit.

chocolate, call your avian veterinarian immediately.

• Avocado should be avoided because it can cause loss of appetite, rapid respiration, excessive preening, bodily irritation, and death. Avocado is considered to be toxic to parrots.

• Other problematic foods include spinach (its high iron content may cause problems with some birds), mushrooms, raw potatoes and onions, and some types of rhubarb. Don't feed your conure uncooked dried lima beans, kidney beans, or soybeans. These raw beans can cause nutritional deficiencies by interfering with chemicals in the conure's system, so be sure to cook them first. Other dried beans are considered to be safe, but you might want to clear them with your avian veterinarian before serving them to your conure.

• Caffeine in any form (soda, coffee, or tea) and alcoholic beverages should *never* be given to conures. Even tiny amounts of alcohol can kill a conure, and caffeine contains substances that cause the avian nervous system to go into overdrive: Respiration speeds up, the heart rate increases dangerously, the kidneys can be affected, and dehydration can occur.

• Though not food items, keep cigarettes, cigars, chewing tobacco, or anything containing tobacco or nicotine out of the reach of a curious conure. Remove or empty any ashtrays, because the cigarette butts are full of deadly nicotine. Ingesting tobacco and nicotine could make your conure sick, cause it to have seizures, or may even kill it.

Special Considerations for Conures

Vitamin A Deficiencies

A conure suffering from a vitamin A deficiency will be prone to allergies, sinus problems, sneezing, dry skin, and possibly hormonal difficulties. Other symptoms include nasal discharge, crusted or clogged nostrils, diarrhea, weight loss, lethargy, dull feathers, depression, loss of appetite, and even bad breath. If your conure shows any of these signs, have your avian veterinarian check it for a vitamin A deficiency. You can help prevent this problem by consistently feeding your conure a well-balanced diet.

Vitamin K

Conures are prone to an unusual bleeding disorder that is caused by a vitamin K deficiency. Vitamin K is essential for conures because it assists the system in blood coagulation, and is necessary for the formation of protein, which assures strong bones and healthy blood and organs. Because they are high in vitamin K, feed your conure plenty of leafy green vegetables, and ask your avian veterinarian if your conure needs calcium or vitamin supplements.

Ultraviolet, or UV, Light

Ultraviolet light is essential for aiding in the conversion of vitamin D_3 from an inactive form to a beneficial one. A hormone, vitamin D_3 works to allow the metabolism of calcium in the avian system. Conures need 12 to 16 hours of UV light a day. A conure deprived of enough UV rays can become ill and might develop weakened bones or an illness similar to rickets in humans. But just because your conure is near a window doesn't mean that it's getting enough of the right kind of light; glass or plastic window panes block almost all UV rays. However, there is something you can do to make sure your conure gets enough beneficial light. Full-spectrum lights and lighting systems with timers can be purchased that will provide the necessary UV rays to keep your conure healthy. Check at your local pet store to see what's available.

Dietary Supplements

If you are feeding your conure a pelleted or extruded diet along with lots of fresh fruits and vegetables, additional dietary supplements won't be needed. Conures receiving a mostly seed diet may need supplements, which are available in powdered formulas or as liquids. Check with your veterinarian before giving your conure any type of dietary supplement.

If a powdered supplement is recommended, sprinkle it onto moist foods such as cottage cheese or fruits. Never add powdered supplements to seeds or processed foods because the powder won't stick and will fall untouched to the bottom of the food cup. You can also mix powdered supplements with water.

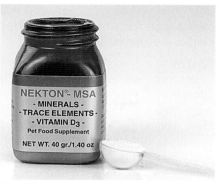

Liquid vitamins.

Note: Water containing vitamins needs to be changed a couple of times a day in order to prevent a buildup of bacteria.

Minerals, Calcium, and Grit

Some conures suffer mineral deficiencies due to improper diets. Minerals and calcium are important for the formation of healthy eggshells and strong bones, especially for breeding hens. You can offer cuttlebones or mineral blocks to provide extra calcium and minerals. Also, these items are just plain fun for conures to chew and also can be an aid in beak grooming.

Wild conures sometimes eat small amounts of gravel, bits of shell, clay, and sand. These materials help grind up seeds and nuts in the gizzard, as well as add minerals to the diet. Because caged conures are fed different diets from those found in the wild, they don't have the same gravel or grit requirements to digest their foods. Unless your avian veterinarian tells you to, don't offer your conure grit; some conures might eat too much and suffer blockages or impactions.

Water

It's the rare conure that isn't a water baby! Unfortunately for you, few busy conures use their water cups just for drinking. Don't be surprised to find toys, bits of paper or tray liner, feathers, and pieces of food deposited in the water cups. Most conures will also use their water cups for bathtubs. Though these habits can be inconvenient for you, your conure needs plenty of fresh, clean drinking water at all times and will quickly suffer from dehydration if deprived. Make sure to thoroughly scrub the water cup every day, because a slimy coat will cover the inside if you don't. You wouldn't want to drink out of such a nasty thing, and you shouldn't expect your conure to, either.

To cut down on the mess, some conure owners switch to water bottles. Water bottles attach to the side of the cage and the conure drinks by licking a ball in the end of a tube extending from the bottle. If you use a drinking bottle, make sure you clean it on a regular basis in order to prevent a buildup of algae on the inside. Check it every day to make sure it's functioning as it should and hasn't become clogged, and scrub it out with a bottle brush. Some resourceful conures outsmart their human companions by learning to shower under their water bottles!

Treats

Show your conure how much you love it by offering a special treat from time to time. Reserve peanuts and sunflower seeds from seed mixes to use as unexpected goodies, and be sure to check out the selection of prepackaged treats made from fruits, nuts, and other wholesome ingredients at your local pet store.

Fun things such as puffed foods, cookie-shaped snacks, and spicy, crunchy nuggets are now available in conure treats, as well as challenging treat-and-toy combinations and interesting items such as pinecones stuffed with seeds, nuts, fruits, and vegetables. Not only are these things tasty treats, but cool toys, as well.

Scan the lists of ingredients in some bird treats and you'll see that they read like a gourmet recipe intended for humans. Among the fruits used are apples, bananas, coconut, papaya, peaches, pineapple, and raisins. Nuts such as almonds, cashews, macadamia nuts,

Stuffed pinecones and chewy birdie cookies are fun treats.

peanuts, pine nuts, pistachios, and walnuts are appealing to conures that enjoy not only the flavor, but love the crunchiness they afford. Popular vegetables include beans, carrots, corn, peas, peppers, rice, and soybeans. Honey is used to add a touch of sweetness to some, and cheddar cheese, oatmeal, peanut butter, peanut butter cookie dough, popcorn, sesame seeds, yogurt, and spicy flavorings are cooked right into others. These treats sound good enough for you to eat, don't they? You should be able to find a great selection of nutritious prepackaged treats at your favorite pet store.

Stubborn conures sometimes accept new foods if they see you eating it.

Tricking a Finicky Eater

Sometimes, no matter what you try, your conure will adamantly refuse to eat the healthy, nutritious foods you offer. A picky eater might toss pellets out of the cage, ignore fruits, or shred but not eat vegetables. If your conure decides to be difficult, try serving up some of those good foods in a special bird bread.

Prepare your favorite cornbread mix (either packaged or your best homemade recipe), and add chopped vegetables such as assorted greens, carrots, cooked beans, squash, corn kernels, yams, sweet potatoes, or broccoli. Stir a handful of pellets or extruded foods into the mix, and don't forget that small chunks of assorted fruits make tasty additions.

Jars of baby food fruits and vegetables can be used instead of fresh, and you can substitute fruit or vegetable juices for any liquids the recipe may call for. Crushed hard-boiled eggs, including the shells, can be added, too. Bake as usual, cool, then serve up in small, conure-sized portions. Unused bread can be frozen for later meals. To feed, simply pull a couple of pieces out of the freezer, thaw, and place in the food dish.

To further tempt your finicky eater, make a show out of eating some of the bread yourself. Rave over how delicious it is and soon your curious conure will just have to have a taste of that wonderful new food. Remember, when introducing healthy, new foods to your conure, persistence is the key. Don't give up on something new if your conure still refuses it after only a few tries. Be as stubborn as your conure!

Chapter Five

Your Conure's Health and Hygiene

Conures are hardy little parrots. As long as yours receives a well-balanced and nutritionally sound diet, stays out of trouble, and avoids accidents, you can expect to share many wonderful years together. Here are some things you need to know in order to give your conure the best chance for a long, healthy life.

The Annual Examination

Regular physical exams are important tools in making sure that your conure stays in the best of health. Potential problems can be headed off, and early signs of disease can be caught in time to start treatment. Your veterinarian will discuss proper nutrition and dietary changes, if necessary, and answer any questions you might have.

• On your first visit, the veterinarian will begin a chart for your conure.

A healthy Jenday conure.

Routine information such as the conure's age, sex, and regular diet will be noted, and a visual exam of the body and feathers will be performed.

• Your conure will be weighed on a gram scale that is outfitted with a perch of some sort, and the weight recorded. Because weight loss is often the first symptom of illness, it's important for the veterinarian to keep careful notes of your conure's normal weight.

• The doctor also will look into its eyes and at the nostrils, beak, and vent, press the keel bone and abdomen, examine the wings, tail, and legs, and listen to the heart and chest.

• Don't be surprised if the veterinarian looks at droppings in the bottom of the transport cage and collects some for tests.

• You will be asked if you want your conure's wings clipped, and the beak or toenails will be trimmed if needed.

• A small amount of blood will be collected for a blood chemistry profile and a complete blood count, and cultures may be taken if your conure seems ill.

All of the above information goes into your conure's permanent health record and will be used in future exams to determine what changes, if any, have occurred.

It's very important to report any changes in your conure's behavior to the veterinarian. Behavior changes are often the first signs that anything is wrong. By being alert to your conure's normal activity, you can help give it the best chance for recovery from illness or injury should anything happen.

The Avian First Aid Kit

Conures, being the bright creatures that they are, can find many ways to injure themselves. Be prepared for the unexpected. By assembling an avian first aid kit and keeping it handy, you won't waste precious time scrambling around trying to find necessary items if your conure gets hurt. Also be sure to tape the phone number of your avian veterinarian near the telephone so you won't have to search for it in an emergency. Don't forget to post an after-hours emergency number, too. You can bet that if your conure is going to need emergency care, it will be after the office has closed for the day or the weekend, or on a holiday!

Here are some items that make up a good first aid kit for the bird room:

- Silver nitrate sticks or styptic powder
- Cornstarch or flour
- Sharp scissors
- Wire cutters
- Tweezers
- Needle-nosed pliers
- Soft, thick towels
- Nail clippers
- Cloth or gauze bandages
- Cotton swabs
- Oral electrolyte replacement fluids

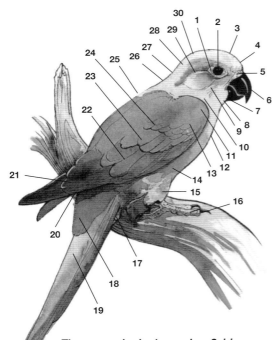

The conure body: 1. eye ring, 2. iris, 3. crown, 4. forehead, 5. cere, 6. upper mandible, 7. lower mandible, 8. chin, 9. cheek, 10. neck, 11. bend of wing, 12. breast, 13. shoulder, 14. abdomen, 15. thigh, 16. toes, 17. undertail coverts, 18. uppertail coverts, 19. tail feathers, 20. rump, 21. primaries, 22. secondaries, 23. greater wing coverts, 24. median wing coverts, 25. back, 26. mantle, 27. nape, 28. back of neck, 29. ear coverts, 30. back of head.

A qualified avian veterinarian will be as familiar with conures as with cockatiels.

• Large plastic syringes (no needles), or eyedroppers
• Heating pad
• Large plastic storage container to hold the items and to double as a hospital area
• Travel carrier

Each of the items in your first aid kit serves a specific purpose. The wire cutters will be necessary should your conure manage to get its leg band caught on a toy, swing, or cage bar. Tweezers are great for removing foreign objects from the eyes or mouth, and you'll need the scissors for cutting away strings or threads that may become entangled around the bird's toes, legs, or other body parts. A supply of clean towels will prove handy for wiping up spills or

droppings, and you can use one to gently restrain your conure, if necessary. Use the bandages for applying pressure, the heating pad to supply warmth, and the cotton swabs to apply any ointments or medications your avian veterinarian may recommend. Needle-nosed pliers are used to remove broken blood feathers, and the travel carrier will be needed if your conure is hurt seriously enough to require a trip to the veterinarian's office.

Silver nitrate sticks will stop bleeding from broken toenails; you can get a supply of these from your veterinarian. If you use styptic powder, be careful that your conure doesn't eat any of it. Use an electrolyte replacement fluid such as

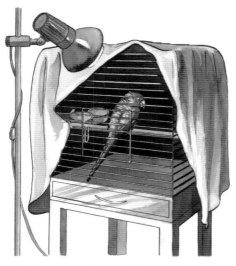

A do-it-yourself hospital cage.

Pedialyte to help a dehydrated bird until medical attention can be administered. If needed, you can gently place a few drops at a time inside the conure's beak with one of the plastic syringes or eyedroppers.

Note: If your conure ever becomes injured, seek medical attention immediately unless the injury is something you can safely handle on your own. You may see various over-the-counter medications and antibiotics at the pet store, but these are seldom effective and can have detrimental results. And never, ever give your conure any medications intended for humans or other pets!

The Hospital Cage

If your conure appears to be ill, don't hesitate to telephone your avian veterinarian immediately. In case of an emergency after the doctor's office hours, or if you need a hospital cage for a recuperating conure, it's a good idea to have one on hand. A hospital cage can be set up easily with items you have around the house. Here is a list of things that will be useful:

- Clean, old towels
- Rolls of paper toweling
- Heating pad
- Blanket
- Sheet
- Small cage or aquarium
- Heavy bowls for water and food
- Lamp
- Thermometer
- Humidifier

To set up a simple hospital enclosure, cover three sides of a cage with a blanket. A smaller cage works best because it will keep your conure from moving around too much, and is easier to heat. Set a lamp nearby and let the warmth of the bulb fill the cage; aim for a temperature of around 85 to 90°F (29.4–32.2°C). Use the thermometer to make sure you don't overheat the hospital area. You also might wish to place a thin sheet over part of the front of the cage to shield the bird from some of the bulb's brightness. If your conure feels like perching, you can place a perch in the lower part of the cage; otherwise, let it sit on a towel in the bottom. Keep your conure covered, heated, and calm. If it will accept a drink, offer electrolyte replenishing fluids, and a couple of favorite treats in case it feels like nibbling on something.

An old aquarium also makes an excellent hospital enclosure for a sick conure. Line the bottom of the tank with a towel and cover it with a thick layer of paper towels to help absorb droppings. Be sure to carefully monitor the appearance of any droppings.

To provide warmth, wrap a heating pad in a thick towel, turn it on a low setting, and place it on top of one end of the tank. You can also use an under-the-tank heater designed for reptile enclosures, positioned under one end of the hospital tank. This way if your conure becomes too warm, it can move away from the heated area. In one end of the tank put a sturdy, untippable bowl of water and another bowl of a favorite food. Carefully set the conure in the tank and cover the top with a blanket. You want to contain as much heat as possible, but you also don't want to overheat your conure. Check the temperature often to make sure it stays steady. You might also want to run a humidifier. Raising the level of humidity in the air aids the conure's system in fighting off infection.

Oversized plastic storage boxes can serve as hospital enclosures for smaller conures. Store all your avian hospital items inside the box and in an emergency situation, everything will be at your fingertips. All you have to do is dump out the supplies, line the box with towels, place the heating pad underneath, and gently set the bird inside. When your conure is feeling better, the plastic box will be quick and easy to clean.

Bleeding Emergencies

Most conures will wreck a blood feather at some time or other in their lives. This can result in what looks like, and can be, a significant blood loss. To help stop the bleeding, apply styptic powder, flour, or cornstarch to clot the blood. (Be careful with the

Broken Blood Feathers

New feathers that are still growing have blood in the shaft and they will bleed if broken or cut. You need to stop the bleeding as soon as possible by removing the broken feather. Ask your avian veterinarian to demonstrate the proper way to remove a bleeding feather so that you'll be prepared in an emergency. Here's how it's done: Have a helper restrain your conure in a towel, being careful not to put pressure on its throat or chest so that its breathing isn't restricted. Then take the needle-nosed pliers from your first aid kit, grasp the broken feather shaft, and with a quick, smooth movement, pull it straight out. If the follicle continues to bleed, press styptic powder, flour, or cornstarch against it and use a folded square of sterile gauze to apply gentle pressure. It should stop soon, but if it keeps bleeding after you've used the clotting agents and applied pressure, take your conure to the veterinarian immediately.

styptic powder; it might burn sensitive skin. Ask your avian veterinarian for advice.) Then gently restrain the conure in a towel and hold pressure on the area with a soft gauze pad until the bleeding stops.

Note: Flour or cornstarch won't clot as quickly as other preparations, so you will need to hold gentle pressure until the bleeding stops.

For bleeding from a damaged toenail, use a silver nitrate stick, or pack the nail with styptic powder, flour, or cornstarch. Apply constant, gentle pressure with a gauze pad or dry washcloth until the bleeding stops. You will probably need to restrain your conure in a towel, being careful not to restrict its breathing. As an alternative, you might scrape the bleeding toenail against a bar of mild, unscented soap to pack the nicked area.

Signs of Poisoning

In some ways, conures are just like children. Anything they find goes straight into their mouths, and it takes only a small amount of a toxic substance to cause poisoning in birds. If you suspect that your conure has been poisoned, don't wait. Call a veterinarian immediately.

Some symptoms of poisoning are breathing problems, disorientation, loss of appetite, vomiting, crouching on the bottom of the cage with ruffled feathers, convulsions, diarrhea, bloody droppings, loss of balance, or falling off the perch. Should your conure show any of these signs, have an avian veterinarian look it over immediately. If you know what your conure ate, be sure to tell the doctor. A conure that has ingested toxic substances may need to be treated by IV fluids, have to be hospitalized, or undergo other drastic measures.

Signs of Illness

In the wild, a sick bird is easy prey and disguising illness is a means of self-preservation. This behavior is referred to as the survival of the fittest, and domestically bred birds are wired to behave in the same way. Usually, by the time a pet bird appears ill, it could have been sick for days. Pay attention to your conure. Any behavior that is not normal for it could mean that it isn't feeling well.

Some common signs of illness are:
• Listlessness
• Dull eyes
• Diarrhea
• Fluffed feathers when it isn't cold or sleeping
• Unsteadiness on the perch
• Crusted nostrils
• Vomiting
• "Clicking" sounds when breathing
• Clumsiness
• Tail bobbing
• Loss of appetite
• Changes in the droppings
• Unusual changes in appearance or behavior

- Sneezing
- Gagging
- Runny eyes or nose
- Swollen eyes
- Weight loss

A sick conure might sit with its eyes closed, or crouch in the bottom of the cage, puffed up and quiet. Its feathers may quiver. A usually vocal conure may stop talking or whistling. Should your conure develop any signs of illness, don't try to treat it yourself. Call an avian veterinarian immediately.

Change in Normal Droppings

Often the first signs of illness will be noticed by a change in the conure's normal droppings. A healthy conure's droppings consist of three components:

1. The green, solid middle part is the fecal matter.

2. Tubes of white urates, or solid urine components, surround the fecal portion.

3. A third component, a clear liquid urine matter can sometimes be observed around the white urates. Since a bird's system automatically conserves water, most urine output will be semisolid.

Note: If your conure's diet consists mainly of extruded or pelleted foods, its feces may be brown instead of the usual green. This is normal, and no cause for alarm.

What if your conure's droppings suddenly change color? Before you panic, think about what may have been on the menu. Dietary changes can affect the appearance of drop-pings. Feeding very moist fruits or vegetables will cause the droppings to be watery; bouts of stress can also cause watery droppings, but these usually clear up when the stress has passed. Some dark-colored foods such as blueberries, pomegranates, beets, or brightly colored extruded foods, can temporarily color the drop-pings. These changes are normal and are no cause for alarm. However, if there have been no changes in the diet and the droppings look signifi-cantly different, there is a chance that your conure is ill. Call your avian vet-erinarian for advice, and be sure to save some of the conure's droppings for examination.

Common Illnesses and Diseases

There are several common ill-nesses and diseases that affect conures, and some of them can be transmitted to humans. If you or a member of your family develop flu- or pneumonialike symptoms when you haven't been exposed to any-thing, it may be wise to visit your physician. Be sure to mention that you have pet birds at home.

To cut the risk of passing a harm-ful bacteria or virus to your conure, shower and change clothes before handling your bird again whenever you have visited another bird, a pet shop, or a bird fair. You can help protect your conure from becoming sick in the first place by educating

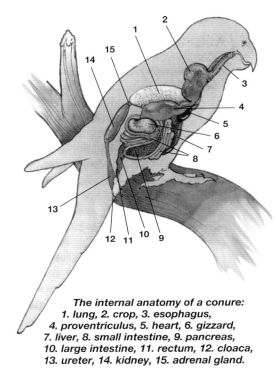

The internal anatomy of a conure:
1. lung, 2. crop, 3. esophagus,
4. proventriculus, 5. heart, 6. gizzard,
7. liver, 8. small intestine, 9. pancreas,
10. large intestine, 11. rectum, 12. cloaca,
13. ureter, 14. kidney, 15. adrenal gland.

caught early enough. Because these symptoms can signal other illnesses as well, tests will need to be performed to ensure an accurate diagnosis and treatment. Sometimes, eating moldy seeds or other old or moldy foods can cause this infection, so feed your conure only fresh foods.

• *Chlamydiosis, also called psittacosis or parrot fever.* This disease was once commonly called parrot fever and you may hear it referred to as psittacosis, ornithosis, or chlamydiosis. Caused by *Chlamydia psittaci*, it is spread by fecal matter, food, and water contaminated by droppings from infected birds, respiratory secretions, and the feather dust of birds with the disease. Infected birds may be carriers but show no symptoms for many years, and the disease can be transmitted to humans. Humans infected with chlamydiosis will suffer pneumonialike symptoms.

While there is no vaccine available at this time, there are reliable tests that can be performed to determine if a bird is infected with chlamydiosis. Blood tests can be used to detect the disease and the bird's feces are usually tested, too. Symptoms include chronic respiratory problems and changes in the appearance of the bird's droppings from a normal color to droppings that are yellow or lime green. If the normally white part of the droppings (the urates) are discolored, it can point to chlamydiosis, but tests must be performed to rule out the possibility of other problems. Drugs are used to combat the disease, and birds can recover. To pre-

yourself about prevention, symptoms, treatments, and cures. Here are some common avian illnesses and diseases you should be aware of. If you think your conure may have any of these conditions, contact your avian veterinarian immediately.

• *Aspergillosis.* Caused by breathing spores of the fungus *Aspergillus fumigatus*, this respiratory infection is manifested by symptoms such as breathing difficulties, tail bobbing, and voice changes. If your conure displays any of these signs, have an avian veterinarian look at it as soon as possible. Aspergillosis can be treated if vent the possible spread of the disease, it is necessary to keep birds that have been affected with chlamydiosis separate from other birds in the home or aviary.

• *Colds.* See Respiratory problems.

• *Conure bleeding syndrome, or CBS.* Conure bleeding syndrome tends to affect mostly baby conures, but adult conures that are severely stressed can be affected as well. Affected conures suffer from a lack of vitamin K.

An insufficient level of vitamin K interferes with normal blood clotting ability, causing abnormal bleeding. CBS is often fatal. Conures treated with extra vitamin K and calcium supplements, and fed diets rich in vitamin K stand a chance of recovery if treatment is begun soon enough. Since conures are so susceptible, a good preventive is to feed a diet that contains high calcium and vitamin K-rich foods. Asparagus, broccoli, Brussels sprouts, cabbage, cauliflower, collard greens, kale, leafy green carrot tops, lentils, lettuce, liver, mustard greens, scrambled eggs, spinach, and turnip greens are recommended foods. If you notice any bleeding in your conure, contact your veterinarian at once.

• *E. coli infections.* Evidenced by runny, diarrhealike droppings that have a strong odor, *E. coli* can be successfully treated if properly identified. It is normally found in human saliva and your conure can become infected by the bacteria if you allow it to take food from your mouth, or if you share open-mouth kisses. To prevent spreading the bacteria, kiss your conure only on the top of the beak and never let it pick your teeth or lick your tongue. If you want your bird to enjoy a snack or meal with you, give it its own dish of food. *E. coli* is also found in other animal saliva. Don't let your dog or cat lick your conure or share food dishes. *E. coli* can be easily treated by antibiotics if caught in time. If you suspect that your conure has an *E. coli* infection, take it to the veterinarian immediately. Rapid diagnosis is the key to successful treatment.

• *Exotic Newcastle disease, or END.* This especially virulent disease can wipe out entire flocks of birds, and has in the past wreaked havoc in the poultry industry. Outbreaks of END can be difficult to contain, and strict quarantine and sanitation procedures must be enforced in affected areas. Some symptoms of END are diarrhea, paralysis, seizures or tremors, sneezing or coughing accompanied by a nasal discharge, or sudden death. END is reportable, and any pet birds affected or exposed are confiscated and put down. Because the disease mostly affects birds that are kept outdoors, most pet birds won't be exposed. To prevent the possible exposure of your conure to END, restrict its access to any outdoor birds, especially if END has been reported in your area. If you suspect that your conure may be infected with END, contact your veterinarian immediately. Unfortunately, an effective treatment for END is not yet available.

• *Diarrhea*. Not to be confused with watery stress droppings, diarrhea can cause an otherwise active conure to become listless and quiet. It may climb down to huddle in the bottom of the cage, where it will sit with fluffed, shivering feathers. Diarrhea should be treated immediately. By the time you notice it, your conure could be seriously ill and dehydrated. There can be several causes for diarrhea, and it's best to have your avian veterinarian look at your conure if it becomes sick. Diarrhea can be a symptom of many illnesses.

• *Giardia*. A microscopic protozoal parasite, giardia is transmitted through contaminated food, water, or fecal material. Symptoms include weight loss, feather plucking, and dry skin. If your bird is diagnosed with giardia, be extra careful when cleaning the cage and avoid touching the droppings of infected birds. Giardia is treatable, but stubborn and often difficult to diagnose. Be especially vigilant with your sanitation and cleaning routines to cut down on the risk.

• *Mites*. Any bird, including conures, can become infested with mites if exposed. The nasty little parasites tunnel into the skin around the eyelids, beak, legs, and feet, and are extremely uncomfortable. If you suspect that your conure has mites, speak with your veterinarian about treatments.

• *Pacheco's disease*. This disease is often associated with conures, macaws, and Amazon parrots, but most species of parrots can catch it.

For some reason, Nanday and Patagonian conures can be carriers of the virus but not show symptoms. Though these are the most common carrier species, many other species can also be carriers. Blood tests can sometimes identify carrier birds shedding the virus.

Also called the psittacine herpes virus, the disease may be tricky to detect and unfortunately, sometimes the first symptoms of Pacheco's is death. The virus may be shed through fecal matter. An affected bird may appear to be lethargic and lose its appetite shortly before dying. Changes in the appearance of droppings or the regurgitation of a clear mucus can be other signs. Pacheco's is often suspect when an apparently healthy bird suddenly dies. Examination of the internal organs during a necropsy (autopsy) sometimes shows the presence of the virus. If a bird is determined to have died from Pacheco's disease, it is important to carefully clean and sterilize anything it may have come in contact with, and to vaccinate any other exposed birds you may have. Human antiviral Acyclovir can reduce the severity of the outbreak and possibly save exposed but not yet seriously ill birds.

• *Psittacine beak and feather disease, or PBFD*. This heartbreaking disease was first thought to be a danger only to cockatoos but is now known to be deadly to all species of parrots. Caused by an airborne virus, PBFD manifests itself with lesions that affect the beak or feathers. Birds infected with PBFD grow deformed feathers, and some birds in advanced stages lose much of their feathering and develop bald patches. Beak abnormalities may also occur.

The virus is spread through contact with the droppings, feather dust, and nasal or oral discharges of infected birds. Once a parrot has contracted the disease, it may take a long time before symptoms emerge, and the bird may become a carrier. Blood tests can be performed to determine if a bird is infected. Sadly, there is no cure yet for PBFD.

• *Psittacine papillomas.* This disease may be caused by a virus similar to the herpes virus associated with Pacheco's disease. South American parrots such as conures, macaws, and Amazon parrots are susceptible to the virus, which causes tumors, warts, or lesions.

Symptoms are growths in the oral cavities, the larynx, esophagus and crop, and the gastrointestinal tracts, usually inside the cloacal openings or vent area. Warts or lesions may also appear on the skin. A sick bird can have breathing difficulties and might strain when defecating.

Birds with this disease can be ill for a long time and suffer serious discomfort. An infected bird's droppings might be loose or show blood, and vent feathers may be matted or stained. Usual treatment is to remove the tumors or warts by cautery and may require several treatments with the unfortunate possibility of recurrence. In some cases, the disease does not appear to spread beyond the cloacal lesions and removing them can allow the bird to live a healthy life with no recurrences. Unfortunately, the bird may still be a carrier. The disease is transmitted only between avians, and not to humans or other animals.

• *Psittacine polyomavirus.* Psittacine polyomavirus is related to the virus that causes tumors or warts in birds, and mainly affects baby parrots. There are different strains of the virus that present different symptoms, but it usually causes feather lesions and abnormal feathers in infected birds. Some symptoms include anorexia, depression, diarrhea, regurgitation, and weight loss. Some birds develop enlarged areas in the abdomen. Vitamin K injections, which aid in blood clotting, can be helpful for birds suffering from slight hemorrhaging. The disease is usually fatal and is very easily spread. There is a vaccine available for at-risk baby birds.

• *Proventricular dilitation disease, also called PDD, or Macaw wasting disease.* Though often called Macaw wasting disease, PDD can affect all species of parrot-type birds and is usually fatal. The disease is thought to be caused by a virus, and scientists are working to isolate the culprit. There is currently no vaccine and no reliable test for the detection of PDD. A treatment has been developed by Dr. Bob Dahlhausen involving human drugs such as Celebrex. While the treatment is experimental, so far it has had very positive results.

Birds affected by PDD can exhibit loss of appetite, vomiting, the passage of whole seeds in the droppings, occasional seizures, paralysis, weight loss, and heart failure. Because neurological symptoms sometimes may be the only ones manifested, misdiagnosis can occur. Due to the fact that food is not digested properly, infected birds appear to starve to death.

• *Respiratory problems.* Because respiratory problems are some of the most commonly seen illnesses in pet birds, many studies have been done to determine causes and treatments. Among the symptoms of a respiratory infection are sneezing, coughing, nasal discharge, weepy eyes, tail bobbing, a clicking noise during breathing, and changes in the voice. Behavioral changes may also occur in usually active conures, such as sitting with ruffled feathers and closed eyes. If your conure exhibits any of these symptoms, have it checked out by an avian veterinarian as soon as possible.

Many things can cause respiratory infections; an all-seed diet that is deficient in vitamin A can pose severe problems. Exposure to various types of bacteria, parasites, and viruses also present risks. It was once thought that drafts caused respiratory infections, but if the bird is fed a nutritious diet and is otherwise in good health, a simple draft shouldn't cause harm unless it is constant and extreme. To avoid problems, don't keep your conure's cage directly beneath a heating or cooling vent.

If your conure develops a respiratory infection, your veterinarian will take swabs of the bird's throat and cloaca, and probably run tests on its droppings. A blood test may be done to rule out the possibility of other diseases. If antibiotics are prescribed for a bacterial infection, be sure to give the entire course of treatment, as instructed by the veterinarian. Should the problem be caused by poor diet, your veterinarian will suggest dietary changes and perhaps prescribe vitamins or other supplements. Depending on what is causing the illness, the treatments could include antifungal medications or antiparasitic preparations. While it's sick, keep your conure warm and as stress-free as possible, and keep it apart from any other birds you may have.

• *West Nile virus, or West Nile encephalitis.* A mosquito-borne illness, pet birds infected with West Nile virus may have diarrhea, lose weight, develop tremors or seizures, experience loss of coordination, or die. To help prevent exposure to mosquitoes, confine your conure inside the house during the hours when mosquitoes are usually active. If you think your conure has West Nile virus, call your veterinarian immediately. The good news is that a vaccine is being developed and will hopefully be available soon. To cut down on the risk of exposing your conure to mosquitos, you can try to reduce the mosquito population by getting rid of any standing or stagnant water on your property, and removing any containers that may collect rainwater.

• *Worms.* Caged birds can occasionally become infested with worms. Roundworms and threadworms are two of the most common types. If you think your conure has worms, have the veterinarian check to make sure. Never give your conure any sort of worm medicine without medical advice. Fortunately, domestically bred conures aren't prone to having problems with worms, as imported conures were. Most captive-bred, indoor conures won't have problems with worms, but these parasites might be a concern to conures housed in outdoor aviaries.

Preventing Disease Transmission at Home

If you have other pets in the home, you have to be extra careful to avoid cross-transmission of any diseases or illnesses. Always wash your hands and change clothes after working with a sick pet. Scrub bowls, utensils, or any items that come in contact with a sick animal in hot, soapy water. Use a solution of hot water and household bleach to sterilize things, and be sure to rinse carefully until all traces of bleach odor or soap are gone. Some common health issues with other pets include the transmission of salmonella from reptiles, pasteurella bacteria from cats, and *E. coli* from mammals, including humans. Pasteurella bacteria is so toxic to conures that even a tiny scratch from a cat can be fatal, and some conures have become ill after simply coming in contact with a cat. To avoid spreading pasteurella bacteria, always wash your hands thoroughly after playing with your cat and before petting your conure.

Don't let your conure eat from the dishes of your other pets, and don't let your other pets lick your conure. Keep your conure from coming in contact with any feces or saliva from other pets.

Diseases can be passed from other birds, too. It's vitally important to quarantine any new birds for the recommended time (30 to 45 days, per your veterinarian's instructions) before introducing them to your existing birds. If you visit a bird show or go to a bird club meeting, always shower and change your clothing as soon as you return home in order to avoid spreading any germs to your conure.

Normal Changes

Conures go through normal, natural changes such as the molting of old feathers, on a regular basis. Their beaks may flake and peel, and the toenails grow long. These are the normal processes of a healthy conure, and are not signs of illness or disease.

Molting

Conures shed their feathers once or twice a year during a natural

Energetic preening removes feather sheaths and grooms the new feathers.

occurrence called molting. This gradual process is the replacement of old, worn feathers with new ones and may take several weeks or longer to complete. A few feathers at a time will be shed, so that the conure doesn't have bald spots or lose too many feathers at once; shedding only a couple of wing feathers at a time ensures that wild conures never lose their ability to fly.

Molting usually takes place at about the same time each year. It's not unusual for conures to look a bit rough or scruffy during a molt. The appearance will return to normal as soon as all the new feathers have grown in and the old, shabby feathers are replaced.

During the molt, it's important to be sure that your conure gets plenty of baths. Without enough moisture, feather sheaths can become very dry and hard and the feathers inside may not develop properly. Affected feathers might not unfurl as they should. If you notice more than one or two odd-looking or deformed feathers during a molt, have your veterinarian check for signs of illness. Dietary problems can also cause feather abnormalities.

Blood Feathers

A conure with a head full of blood feathers, or pinfeathers, looks a little like a porcupine. The new feathers grow in encased in a hard, white keratin sheath and are very sensitive. A blood vein running through the sheath nourishes the growing feather and as the feather develops, the outer sheath dries and flakes off.

Conures preen their feathers to remove the dried sheaths and open the new feathers. You'll notice a lot of white, flaky material during this time, and it may appear that your conure has a bad case of dandruff! Don't be alarmed; this is just the powder from the dried sheaths. Because your conure can't reach its head or the back of its neck to preen away the sheaths, it will appreciate a little help from you. Make sure the sheaths aren't concealing blood feathers, then carefully scratch away the dried material with a fingernail. Should you accidentally press too hard on a new feather, you'll probably receive a nip on the finger. New blood feathers can be touchy.

Molting Moodiness

Your conure might seem a bit cranky or moody during the molting season. New feathers can be sensitive and uncomfortable, and the accompanying itchiness can make your normally cuddly conure want to avoid being touched. Help make things easier by providing lots of warm baths and an extra-healthy diet. Ask your veterinarian about supplements if your conure isn't on a pelleted or extruded diet. You may need to feed a little extra protein, vitamins, or minerals during the molt.

Plenty of rest is important for your conure while it is molting, and at least 10 to 12 hours of darkness a night is recommended. Growing all those new feathers can be stressful, and covering part of the cage during the day will allow the conure to have a quiet place to rest and feel secure. Don't let anyone tease your conure during the molt; already sensitive, the added anxiety could cause a nervous bird to start feather picking. A conure under a lot of stress may have a more difficult molt and may shed an abnormally high number of feathers.

Personal Grooming

Healthy conures that receive a well-rounded, nutritious diet and are kept in a clean environment usually won't require extensive grooming. Things such as beak trimming and toenail and wing clipping can be done during regular veterinary

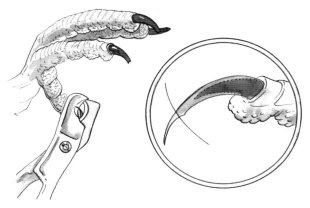

With sharp clippers, snip off just the tip of the nail.

checks. You can even learn to do some of the grooming yourself.

Nail Clipping and Filing

You can have your veterinarian clip your conure's nails, but you can clip them at home if you know how. Using a sharp set of clippers, carefully snip off just the pointed tip of the nail. Don't clip too much or you risk nicking the blood vessel, or *quick,* that runs nearly to the end of the nail. Some conures have light-colored toenails that make it easy to see the vein inside. For dark-colored or black toenails in which the vein can't be seen, be sure to clip only the very tip to avoid bleeding. Some conures can be trained to stand on a tabletop or on your lap and let you clip their nails. If your conure resists the chore, you will probably have to restrain it in a towel.

If restraint is necessary, gently wrap the conure in a soft towel and pull out a foot. Uncurl the toes (which will probably be clenched in a tight fist), and be careful not to nick the foot or toe with the clippers. Have someone help you, if necessary, and always have your avian first aid kit standing by in case a toenail starts to bleed.

Note: When restraining your conure, be very careful not to put pressure on its chest, upper abdomen, or throat because doing so will restrict its breathing.

Filing the nails can be turned into a game for some conures. Let your conure play with an emery board and gently rub the board against the tip of the nail. If your conure gets into the habit of having its nails filed, it will be extremely easy to keep them groomed. You might also install a couple of concrete perches or mineral blocks in the cage for your conure to climb on. This will help keep toenails from becoming too long.

The proper way to restrain a conure in a soft cloth.

Beak Grooming

It's normal for layers of the beak to peel occasionally, and some birds will let you gently scratch the flaky sections off with a fingernail. Blue-crowned conures especially are notorious for the needle-sharp points that sometimes grow on the tips of the upper beak.

To help your conure groom its beak, try offering a concrete perch or a lava block. Conures will sometimes use these items to wipe wet foods off the beak and this will naturally wear the beak down on its own. You should never try to trim the beak yourself unless you have been trained to do so. If your conure's beak looks extremely overgrown, see your avian veterinarian. Sometimes, overgrown beaks can signal health problems.

Wing Clipping

For safety's sake, it is a good idea to keep your conure's wings clipped. Clipping the flight feathers isn't cruel or painful, and could save your conure's life by restricting its ability to fly out of open windows or doors, or into closed windows, mirrors, ceiling fans, fireplaces, containers of water, or hot stoves. Some people prefer to let their birds remain flighted, and these people have to be extra vigilant in order to avoid accidents. While it is up to the owner to decide whether or not to clip, conures with clipped wings are less likely than flighted birds to be involved in injury-sustaining accidents. You may also find that your conure is better behaved and easier to handle when its wings are kept neatly clipped.

If you would like to clip your conure's wings yourself, first have an experienced person such as a veterinarian or bird groomer teach you how. It isn't a difficult task, but it can be scary if you don't know what you're doing.

Some very tame and easily handled conures will stand still and hold their wings out to be clipped. For a conure that must be restrained, it's a good idea to enlist a helper. Be careful not to restrict the bird's breathing while holding it in a towel, then gently extricate a wing and fan out the feathers. With a pair of sharp scissors, clip the first seven or eight primary flight feathers; these are the feathers on the outside edge of the wing. Be careful not to clip them too short, and don't clip blood feathers. You can easily identify blood feathers—they will have a white coating with a dark blue coloration underneath. Be sure to trim the flight feathers on both wings, and keep the first aid kit handy in case of an accident.

Never clip your conure's wings too severely. Cutting too many feathers can cause problems such as loss of balance, and broken tail feathers or other injuries from crash landings. Should a conure fall from its perch or playstand, it depends on its wing feathers to help it land. A properly clipped conure will glide to the floor instead of dropping like a rock. The wing feathers will grow back in after each molt and should be checked periodically to see when another trimming is needed.

Bathing

If given the opportunity, most conures will bathe regularly, and in fact will often splash out all their drinking water. Frequent baths help keep the feathers and skin in good condition, and also provide entertainment for water-loving conures. Though conures and water seem to go together, there are some conures that don't enjoy bathing. A thorough misting from a spray bottle will provide a fine bath for them.

Purchase a large plastic bottle with a spray attachment and clearly mark it to be used for your conure only. Never use a spray bottle that has previously contained chemicals because there may be harmful residue left inside. To give your conure a shower, fill the bottle with tepid or cool water and gently mist the bird until its feathers are soaked. Avoid

Carefully fan out the wing feathers and clip the first seven to eight primary flights.

A Nanday and a Sun conure sharing a bath.

squirting directly into your conure's face. If the conure reacts with fear to the spray bottle, find another way to allow it to bathe.

Showers: Some people take their conures into the shower with them. If the thought of claws digging into your shoulder doesn't appeal to you, there are perches available that attach by suction cup to the wall of the shower. When showering with your conure, be careful not to get soap or shampoo on its feathers, and adjust the spray so that the water isn't pelting too forcefully. It's best not to use very hot water in order to avoid burning your conure or drying out its skin.

Bathtubs: A heavy, round glass pie plate makes an excellent bathtub for conures. Fill it with an inch or so of cool water and let your conure climb inside. You might want to place a few towels around to catch any water that will be splashed out of the bath. Bathtubs and sinks also are great for bathing, as long as you are there to supervise. You might have to experiment to see which method best suits your conure. Some conures even love rolling around in a bed of wet spinach or lettuce leaves.

After the Bath

After a bath or shower, your normally beautiful conure will look like a matted-up bundle of shivering feathers. While you may be shocked by its appearance, don't be concerned by the shivering—shivering is a normal reaction that helps to expand the wet down feathers and to create body heat. Make sure your conure is in a warm, draft-free area so that it will dry quickly.

Some conures enjoy being dried by a hair dryer set on low heat and held at a safe distance. This can be a fun game as long as the conure doesn't get overheated or stressed by the hair dryer. A thorough preening session usually follows a bath and your conure will soon regain its lovely appearance.

Chapter Six

Conure Cages and Accessories

Choosing the right habitat for your conure involves much more than simply going to the store, picking out a pretty cage, taking it home, and expecting everybody to be happy with it. Not only must the cage be suitable for your conure, but you'll want it to look nice and fit well in your home, too. Any good pet or bird specialty store, and quite a few department stores, carry cages suitable for conures. Cages can also be ordered from many avian publications and Internet web sites that carry bird supplies and accessories. Keep the following suggestions in mind as you shop, and you'll be better able to choose the perfect cage for your conure, and for your home.

Cage Sizes and Styles

Your conure will thank you if you purchase the largest cage you can afford. Think of it this way: You wouldn't want to spend a lot of your time cooped up in a tiny room the size of a closet, so you shouldn't expect your conure to be happy in a cage that's too little to allow for freedom of movement. Of course, if you plan to allow your conure a lot of time outside the cage, then a smaller cage can be used for sleeping and eating.

Keep in mind that conures have long, pointed tail feathers that need plenty of room to avoid being crushed or damaged. A good minimum size for a conure cage would be around 18 inches (46 cm) square for the smaller *Pyrrhura* species, while larger conures such as Patagonians, *Aratingas*, and Nandays will be happy in cages that measure at least 24 inches (61 cm) square. Select a cage that will allow your conure to fully extend its wings without touching the sides of the cage, and that is roomy enough to allow it to comfortably perch with plenty of head and tail feather room. Make sure your conure can't get its head stuck between the bars, and that it can't slip through bars that are spaced too far apart. Cage bars that are spaced ½ inch to ¾ inch (12.7–19 mm) apart are suitable for most conures. Examine the cage you like to determine that the bar spacing used is appropriate for your conure.

Shapes

Square cages, round cages, pagoda-shaped cages—you name it; you can probably find a cage in that style. But if the cage you choose is inappropriate for your conure, then no matter how pretty it is, neither you nor your bird will be happy.

Round cages: Round cages are not good choices because your conure has no corners to escape to if it feels threatened. And unless the round cage is quite large, there won't be as much room inside as a square or rectangular cage would provide. It can be difficult to place perches inside a round cage so that a conure's long tail feathers aren't crushed, and so that droppings don't collect on the perches or fall into the cups. Round cages can be awkward for a conure to climb around in, too.

Bars: Because conures are climbers by nature, horizontal bars are much more suitable for them than vertical bars, which can be difficult to climb. And while cockatiel cages will serve for some of the smaller *Pyrrhura* conures, the bigger conures, such as Patagonian conures and most of the *Aratinga* species, need roomier homes. Full-sized parrot cages wouldn't be too large at all for these active birds.

Solid tops: Most cages have bars across the tops, but some designs have solid tops. Though they might be attractive, you might want to pass on a solid-topped cage, for several reasons. Solid tops sometimes distress conures that don't like anything hovering over their heads. Another reason? Conures love to climb and most enjoy hanging upside down from the top of the cage. A solid-topped cage would prevent this type of exercise.

Rectangular or square cages are excellent choices for active conures.

Cages with horizontal bars are great for climbing parrots such as conures.

Remember: Whatever size and style of cage you decide on, make sure that it provides ample space for perches, toys, and food and water cups, is safe, and offers lots of room for your busy conure's activities.

Cage Materials and Finishes

Before spending money on an expensive cage, find out what it's made of and be sure that it is safe for your conure. Those pretty bamboo cages are poor choices for conures, or for any parrot-type bird. Their powerful beaks would make splinters of bamboo in no time. Brass, copper, lead, and zinc are dangerous for any pet bird. Because conures love to chew and will often gnaw on the cage bars, cages made of these materials can present life-threatening hazards because of the possibility that the materials might be nibbled off and ingested. Wrought iron is an attractive and popular material for cages, and stainless steel cages are indestructible and heavy.

Conure-appropriate cages are available in a wide variety of pretty, stylish colors that are finished with bird-safe paint. There are also powder-coated cages that work well for conures. Powder-coating is a dry finishing process that can be used on a variety of materials and is available in a multitude of lovely colors.

Cages that are powder-coated are durable, rust-resistant, and hold up well to conure beaks.

Used Cages

You might sometimes run across used cages, and these can be real bargains. But before you purchase a used cage, find out what happened to its previous occupant. Can the cage be sterilized if the bird died from an illness? If you're not sure, pass it up. Beware, too, of repainted cages, especially for hookbills. A conure's sharp beak can easily flake off bits of paint that might then be swallowed. If you plan to buy a used cage that has been refinished, try to find out what sort of paint was used, and verify that it was lead-free. To be safe, consider refinishing the cage yourself, using materials you know are lead-free. It doesn't take much lead in any form to cause serious health problems, or possibly death, in conures. And of course, you'll want to check out any accessories that come with the cage. If you find anything that is of questionable material, remove it before allowing your conure inside the cage, and certainly replace all perches or toys.

Safety Considerations

Make sure there are no sharp edges anywhere in or on the cage, and that all doors and hinges work smoothly. Check the welding and bars for any problems, and look for

Roomy wire cage.

any joinings or spaces that could trap a conure's toe or beak tip. All weldings should be lead-free. If the cage you are interested in has any openings a curious conure could possibly get its head stuck in, pass on that cage and find another that has no unsafe areas. Birds have died of strangulation after getting their heads caught in cages with incorrectly spaced bars, and from becoming trapped in openings from which they couldn't free themselves.

Doors and Hinges

Whatever type of doors the cage has, check carefully to make sure there are no sharp edges that could cut your conure (or you), and that there are no tricky spots that could snag a toenail. The door should open and close smoothly, and should fasten securely.

Some cage designs feature doors that open by sliding up and down. If you choose a cage like this, make sure that these doors are always fastened when open so that they can't fall down and injure a conure that is climbing in or out of the cage. A falling door could cause injuries such as fractures or broken bones, and a conure caught in a falling door would more than likely thrash around in a panic and injure itself even more severely. In extreme cases, the door could kill one of the smaller conures by breaking its neck. If you decide to purchase a cage with this type of door, don't take chances. Always make certain to secure it with a twist tie or other bird-safe fastener when open so that it can't fall on your conure.

Note: Keep in mind that this type of door can also be easily opened by a determined conure! Secure it closed to make sure that your conure doesn't escape when you aren't looking.

Look for cages that have wide doors that will allow easy access to the inside of the cage for cleaning, and for taking your conure out of the cage. Some cages have "landing" doors that allow a conure to perch on them when the doors are open.

Outside Access Feeders

If the cage you choose has outside access food and water cups, make sure your conure can't get its head caught between the cups and the cage bars. The fastening mechanisms on these openings should operate smoothly and fit well enough so that the conure can't manipulate them into opening. Some smart conures can learn how to jiggle the closures so that they can open them, push or pull the cups out, and then escape. If your conure tries this, you may want to invest in some small, bird-safe fasteners that can be used to secure the access areas. Never underestimate the creativity and determination of a conure!

Do-it-Yourself Perches and Wooden Toys

Chewing is a favorite conure hobby, and they adore wooden items that they can destroy. Did you know that you can make your own

Green-cheek perched on an open cage door.

cage accessories, such as perches and chewable toys, from nontreated wood? If you decide to try this, make certain that you don't use pressure-treated wood in anything you make for your conure. Why? Because this type of lumber contains CCA, a chemical that prevents the wood from rotting and from becoming infested with insects. The chemical is dangerous to birds because it contains arsenic. Once ingested, arsenic can build up to dangerous levels in a bird's system, causing serious health problems or even death. Non-pressure-treated wood is safe for conures, and can be bought at the

A variety of food and water cups are available.

same locations as pressure-treated. Double-check before purchasing to make sure you are getting non-pressure-treated wood.

Setting Up the Cage

Outfit your conure's cage with its comfort in mind. There should be ample cups for fresh water, food, and treats, plenty of comfortable perches, an interesting array of toys, and still lots of room for the conure.

Food and Water Cups

The new cage you purchase will include cups, but they may not be to your conure's preference. If this turns out to be the case, head back to the store to check out what's available. You'll find that there are several different types of food and water cups from which to choose. The most commonly used materials are ceramic, stainless steel, and heavy plastic. If your conure is a dedicated chewer, lightweight plastic cups may not be a good option unless you don't mind buying new ones all the time.

Keeping Cups Clean

It doesn't take long for bacteria to build up in a dirty water cup, or in one used for serving up soft foods. Make sure you clean any messes from the water cups as soon as possible, especially if your conure is one of those birds that likes to dunk its food in the water. This leads to an unappetizing mess that will rapidly turn smelly and bacteria-laden. If your conure is a food-dunker, you will find that the water needs to be dumped and replenished several times a day. Never let the dirty water sit too long—not only will it look and smell bad, but it could make your conure sick.

Having two sets of cups is helpful. One set can be cleaned and sterilized while the other is in use. To clean your conure's dishes, wash them in hot, soapy water and rinse thoroughly. You can use household bleach to sterilize them, but be sure to rinse away all traces of bleach before returning them to the cage. If you can still smell bleach after rinsing, rinse again until all the odor is gone. You can also use a dishwasher to clean the bird's dishes as you wash your family's dishes. The detergent and hot water will safely sterilize the cups.

The Bottom of the Cage

Because conures are so messy, a cage with a slide out bottom tray will be easier to clean than one with a stationary bottom. Avoid cages with sloping bottom sides. The slanted sides tend to catch droppings and can be difficult to keep clean. Cages with grates help keep playful conures from walking around in the mess on the bottom of the cage. Unfortunately, the grates also tend to catch droppings. You can buy products at your pet store that will help keep droppings and food debris from sticking to grates and cage bars.

Keep the grate clean by regularly scrubbing away caked-on messes. If you intend to use litter or some sort of bedding material in the bottom of the cage instead of paper, then be sure to purchase a cage with a grate so that your conure won't be able to reach the litter. Some of the litter or bedding can be harmful to your conure if it happens to eat any of the material.

Cage Liners

You will need to line the bottom of the cage with something to collect droppings, discarded food, toys, and feathers. What you decide to use is a matter of convenience for you, and of safety and sanitation for your conure.

Many conures like to perch on the cups while eating.

Paper or Litter?

Basic black newsprint is nontoxic and can even help inhibit the growth of some types of bacteria. Some lighter-colored conures (such as Suns or Jendays) that like to play on the bottoms of their cages might get a bit dingy looking, but the newsprint is harmless and will wash off. If your conure is a habitual chewer, don't let it shred or chew brightly colored papers. The ink contains chemicals, some of which could be toxic to birds. As an alternative to newspaper, some conure keepers line the bottoms of the cages with waxed

Types of Shavings

Never use cedar shavings in the bottom of your conure's cage or in its sleeping area. Aromatic cedar smells wonderful, but it emits a chemical called plicatic acid that can be harmful to conures. Likewise, pine shavings contain an irritant called abietic acid that could irritate the sensitive respiratory systems of some conures. Kiln-dried shavings may be safer. If any shavings or bedding materials emit a strong odor, don't use them.

paper, butcher paper, or brown paper bags.

Change the cage paper every day or so. Don't let a buildup of droppings and old food accumulate—not only is this unsightly, but it is unhealthy as well. Bacteria will rapidly multiply in the debris, especially in warm temperatures, and could possibly make your conure, or you, sick. In the wild, conures can fly away from their messes. Because this isn't possible for pet conures, it is up to you to keep their habitats as clean as can be.

Litter and Bedding Materials

Many different materials are used to make cage bedding or litter. Ground-up walnut shells, compacted shredded paper, corncobs, and wood shavings are all common ingredients. While considered safe for use around pet birds, be sure that your conure doesn't eat any of the material. It could cause digestion problems, intestinal blockages, or in some cases, death.

Cob bedding or other litter material may be more convenient to clean but can hide the conure's droppings. Sometimes, the first signs of illness are detected when the owner notices a change in the bird's droppings; keep this in mind should you decide to use litter instead of paper in the bottom of the cage. Also, some conures are "flappers" and a lot of their bedding or litter may end up outside the cage on your floor, instead of inside the cage protecting the bottom of it.

Whatever litter or bedding material you decide to use, make sure you change it on a regular basis to avoid odors, a dangerous buildup of bacteria-producing waste, and spoiled food.

Perches

Perches come in many different shapes, sizes, and materials. There are oval, round, square, and flat perches. They can be made from natural wood, PVC pipe, plastic, acrylic, dowel rods, or even colorful cement. Conures spend most of their time on their feet (except for when they are clinging to the cage bars by their beaks, or rolling around on their backs) and they need comfortable furniture for eating, sleeping, and playing. Offer perches in several different sizes and materials so that your conure has a choice of where

Mitred conures on PVC perch.

to sit or sleep. It's a good idea to provide differently-sized perches, but make sure that each is of appropriate size and shape for your conure's feet.

Perch covers: While shopping for cage accessories, you may notice that many stores carry sandpaper perch covers. While these items are supposed to be helpful in maintaining proper toenail length, constant use can make a conure's feet sore. If you wish to use these covers, think about using them on only one perch, and leave the other perches unwrapped.

Lava rocks and cement perches: You might also consider providing a lava rock for your conure to climb around on, or giving it a cement perch. The rough surface of cement perches helps keep the conure's toenails filed down, and can aid in beak grooming, too. These perches come in several shapes and colors, so keep your conure's size and color preferences in mind while choosing. To encourage your conure to use its new cement perch, place it near the water cup so that the conure will have to stand on it to drink. Use only one or two cement perches in the cage. While they are good grooming aids, they shouldn't be the only perches offered, as too frequent use might cause foot problems or discomfort later on.

Cleaning the Perches

Perches will get dirty from time to time and will need to be cleaned.

Perch Size

Observe your conure as it rests and pay careful attention to how its feet fit the perch. Ideally, a conure's foot should encircle about one half to two thirds of the perch. If its front toes can circle all the way around to the back toes, then the perch is too small. You should make sure that the perch isn't too wide, either.

Note: A wide perch gives your conure the option of standing flat-footed and can provide a welcome variety in places to sit. Just make sure that it isn't the only perch your conure has. Perches that don't fit a conure's foot comfortably can cause pressure points that can lead to sores, tired feet and legs, or painful cramps.

Plastic, cement, or PVC perches can be washed in hot soapy water to which a small amount of household bleach has been added. To clean wooden perches, scrape them thoroughly with a perch scraper (available at any pet store), or with sandpaper. Never use bleach on wooden perches as it doesn't rinse out of the porous wood.

Helpful tip: Pick up an extra set of perches to have on hand to use when you need to clean the soiled ones.

Using Tree Branches for Perches

Natural wooden branches make great perches—conures love to strip the bark from them! Some woods considered safe to use are ash, aspen, beech, birch, cottonwood, dogwood, elm, fir, magnolia, manzanita, mulberry, pine, and poplar. Avoid using branches from certain fruit trees, especially cherry, crab apple, peach, pear, plum, and nectarine because the bark from some fruit trees contains cyanide-producing compounds. These substances are toxic to birds. Also avoid using branches that are covered with sticky sap. If you are in doubt about the safety of any type of natural branches, ask your veterinarian or call your local plant nursery.

If you plan to harvest the branches yourself, steer clear of using branches from roadside trees; these trees could be contaminated with a buildup of dangerous chemicals and exhaust residue. Also make sure that the trees haven't been sprayed with pesticides. Choose trees only from locations you know to be free from any chemicals or treatments.

Once you have found safe branches, clean them thoroughly to get rid of dirt, debris, wild bird droppings, and any bugs that might be hidden in the bark. Branches can be cleaned with hot, soapy water to which you have added a small amount of household bleach. Scrub the branches with a stiff brush, rinse until no trace of bleach odor or soap remains, and leave outside in the sun until the branches are completely dry.

Position the branches in the cage so that your conure can climb on them but still have space to move around freely. Not only will your conure enjoy stripping the bark from natural wooden branches, but it will also enjoy reducing the limbs to toothpicks. Keep a supply of safe, cleaned branches available to replace worn-out or destroyed perches as needed.

Perch Placement
• Be sure you don't place one perch directly below another or you will constantly be scraping off droppings!
• Don't situate perches over water or food cups or the contents will be soiled.
• Be careful to allow plenty of room between the perches and the cage bars to avoid the possibility of crushing your conure's tail feathers. Constant contact with the cage bars will result in ragged feathers.

Green-cheeks perched on a natural tree branch.

Toys and Accessories

Conures are wild and crazy birds! They appreciate having a variety of colorful, interesting toys to beat up and play with. Anything that can be chewed to bits is great fun for their busy beaks. But conures can become bored if they have to play with the same old toys every day. Keep several types of playthings on hand so that you can rotate them to prevent boredom.

If your conure seems afraid of new toys, introduce the toys slowly by placing them on a nearby table where your conure can get used to looking at them. While it is watching, enthusiastically play with the toys and let it see what a great time you're having. Before long, your conure's natural curiosity will win out and it will have to have a go at the toy, too.

Note: Don't try to rush your conure into accepting things that it is uncomfortable with. Be patient, take your time, and soon you and your conure will be both be happy with the new things.

Toys will need to be cleaned from time to time. They get grimy from droppings and splashed-on food,

Conures appreciate a wide variety of toys!

Conure Favorites

Stainless steel bells are longtime conure favorites. Just make sure that the clapper is lead-free and can't be removed by a determined conure. Swings, stainless steel chains, smooth cotton rope toys, untreated wooden blocks, and chemical-free rawhide toys are great distractions for busy conures. If you're planning to use any type of chain, make sure the links are smooth with no rough edges, that there are no openings to catch a conure's toenail or beak tip, and that the length of the chain is short enough that a playful conure can't loop it around its body and become entrapped.

Conures enjoy ripping paper into tiny bits, so save your junk mail for your conure to "read." The subscription cards that fall out of magazines are great for conures. Just be careful not to use any of the heavily perfumed cards that come in some publications. Ripping apart clean paper coffee filters, paper napkins, and paper towel and toilet paper rolls is fun, too, but supervise this activity to make sure your conure doesn't get its head or body caught inside the roll. Birds have died after becoming stuck inside, falling into water cups, and drowning. And those hard plastic soda bottle caps make cool toys. Some conures enjoy using them for scoops or cups, and will eat out of them!

Many conures enjoy swings. When choosing a swing for your conure, look for one that allows plenty of head and body room and

and from being regurgitated on by the conure. Wash them with hot soapy water and rinse well. Wooden toys can't be cleaned as easily and will probably need to be replaced instead. Rope toys can be tossed into the washing machine, but should be replaced as they get worn to prevent toenails from becoming trapped in the loose threads. Leather or rawhide toys will need to be replaced periodically.

A playful Blue-crown.

Green-cheek on swing.

that is equipped with a comfortable perch. Conures love to swing wildly back and forth, screeching and squawking the whole time. Though it might not be too pleasant an experience for the human members of the family, remember that your conure is having the time of its life.

Playstands and Playgyms

Energetic conures that are allowed a lot of time outside the cage enjoy romping on specially designed playstands and playgyms. These items can be handy places to perch your conure while you are

doing chores, watching television, cleaning the bird cage, or having dinner with the family. This way the conure can be right in the middle of the action, but still safely out of the way. Choose a playstand design that has places to attach toys, swings, and food and water cups. A tray at the bottom to catch droppings and other messes will help keep your floor clean.

There are many models of playstands on the market. Made from anything from PVC pipe to wood, these items are available at pet stores, and by mail order from avian-related publications and Internet shopping sites. Most come equipped with perches, toys, and trays. Some

Playstands are fun for conures and their human friends!

T-stand.

Do-it-Yourself Playstands

If you are good with tools, you can build a customized playstand yourself. You'll need a couple of pieces of PVC pipe, and several T- and elbow joints.

• Decide how big or elaborate you want the stand to be, then sketch out your design so you have something to go by.

• Using a hacksaw, cut the pipe into the lengths you need, then slip the PVC pipe pieces into the joints. The pieces should fit snugly together.

• Before you let your conure onto its new play area, make sure the finished stand is steady and won't tip over. To keep the pipe from being too slippery for your conure's feet, rough it up with sandpaper or a hacksaw, and carefully remove any bits of plastic that might be eaten by your conure.

Note: Don't use any sort of glue on the pipe, as it could be toxic to your conure.

playstands even feature natural wood perches.

There are also cage-top playgyms that fasten to the bars. Some of them are quite elaborate, while others consist of a simple perch with a cup. T-stands are popular with many conure keepers. These consist of a single upright pole, with a crossbar at the top for the bird to perch on. Cups, toys, and swings can be attached, and some T-stands have trays underneath the crossbar to catch droppings and other messes.

Cage Covers

A bedtime cage cover provides not only privacy for your conure, but a sense of security, as well. A cover will keep the cage warm at night, will filter out bright light, and give your conure a chance to rest without distractions. An added bonus: A good cover for the cage may also allow you to have a few extra minutes of sleep in the morning before your conure wakes up and greets the day.

Choose a smooth fabric that doesn't have a lot of loose strings that your conure could become entangled in, and avoid weaves that could catch toenails. Dark colors that block light will provide the most privacy, while a brightly patterned print might be too stimulating for conures, since these birds perceive and react to colors.

Cage covers can be purchased in pet stores, from bird magazines, and from on-line bird supply shopping sites. If you have a sewing machine, you can also make your own cage covers. Suitable materials can be found in fabric stores or department stores, and even in the bed linens section. A large sheet will drape comfortably over most cages, and can be cut and hemmed to fit.

Not all conures like to be covered at night, and it's not really a necessity to cover them. Observe your conure to see how it reacts when it's time for bed. Should it seem to be frightened of the dark, it may appreciate a small night light in the room. If it likes the cover but seems anxious, leave the cage cover open a bit so that your conure can see some light. Your conure will let you know what makes it comfortable.

Location of the Cage

Conures are highly social creatures that crave consistent interaction with their flock. You can't put a conure in the back room by itself and expect it to be happy. A well-adjusted and well-socialized conure will be happiest where it can see its human family members and take part in the activities.

• You will need to find a comfortable spot that is not in direct sunlight, and not right over or under a heating or air conditioning vent.

• There should be plenty of space around the cage to avoid bumping or jostling by people passing through the room, and the cage must be in a stable location where it can't be knocked over.

• Most conures appreciate a wall behind at least one side of the cage.

• Make sure there are no items within reach of the conure that could be dangerous, such as the ties from miniblinds, electrical cords and plugs, telephone cords, or items containing lead, such as some lamps, decorations, or lead crystal.

- Avoid placing the cage near windows or exterior doors, especially if they are not screened. Not only is this area drafty, but there is the danger that other animals could sneak inside and get to your conure.
- Don't keep your conure's cage next to an uncurtained window. Direct sunlight coming straight through a window can quickly cause a conure to become overheated.
- While the kitchen may seem to be a suitable area for your conure's cage, it is not the best location. There are too many dangers in the kitchen. Hot stoves or gas burners, pans of boiling water or cooking food, fumes from nonstick cookware, hot grease, scalding steam, soapy dishwater, or chemical cleaners are all dangerous to conures. If you have to keep your conure in the kitchen, make sure that it is never allowed out of its cage unsupervised. It would take only a few seconds for something terrible and irreversible to happen.

Keeping Things Clean

It's a fact of life—if you live with a conure, you live with mess! Conures enjoy pushing things such as bits of fruit or vegetables, wads of shredded newspaper, or small toys out through the cage bars. And since some conures love to cling to the sides of the cage, you can bet that the cage bars will become festooned with droppings. Needless to say, that shiny, pretty cage and the area around it will eventually be in need of a good cleaning. But don't panic. There are things you can do to keep the mess under control.

Ten Tips for Easy Cleaning

1. Invest in a hand-vac. If you can afford it, pick up one of those small portable hand-vacuum cleaners. They make quick cleanup a breeze and will save you hours in intensive vacuuming. By allowing you to immediately grab up dry messes such as spilled seeds or pellets, not only will the area around the cage look better, but your whole house will feel cleaner. If you can't afford a hand-vac, a small whisk broom and dustpan works great, too.

2. Wipe up spills immediately. Conures love to play in their water and nothing within reach is safe! Keep a roll of absorbent paper towels near the cage to wipe up water or blotches of wet foods. They're handy for wiping up droppings, too.

3. Keep a stack of clean newspapers or the cage liner of your choice handy. It's much easier and quicker to clean when you don't have to scramble around looking for something to use in the bottom of the cage. Stash the materials in a box or basket under the cage for easy access.

4. Place a clear vinyl runner beneath cages to keep carpets or flooring clean. You can purchase clear vinyl material in most department or flooring stores. Vinyl office desk mats work well, too. If you want to add a splash of color, you can pick up shower curtains in a variety of pretty patterns. Not only do these things help keep your floor splatter-free, but they are easy to clean and can be cut to the size you need.

5. Keep a spray bottle of plain water near the cage. Quickly spritz messes to make cleaning easier. Harder dried-on messes can be treated with one of the spray-on cage cleaner preparations you can find at the pet store. Follow the directions on the package.

6. Be careful where you position food and water cups. By placing cups lower in the cage, you can minimize the amounts of seeds, pellets, or other foods that wind up on the floor. Just take care to not place the cups where your conure will defecate in them.

7. Use cage skirts or aprons. Many companies make cage skirts. These are usually constructed of fabric or plastic, and attach around the lower part of the cage with Velcro or elastic. If your conure likes to chew, make sure it can't reach the skirt. Other options are metal or hard plastic aprons that fasten to the cage bars and deflect messes back into the bottom of the cage.

8. Deep-clean dirty cages in the shower. For a more intensive clean-ing, first remove your conure from the cage along with any wooden perches, toys, cups, leather or wood items, and all the cage liner. Then set the cage in the shower, turn on the hot water, and scrub the cage all over with a stiff brush. Be sure to get between all the bars and into any crevices and hinges. Rinse well, let air dry, and replace the accessories. Oh, and don't forget to let the conure back in!

9. Don't position cages too close to walls. If you must place your conure's cage up against a wall, first cover the wall with clear acrylic sheets or contact paper. Most department or hardware stores carry these items. You can also paint the wall with water-resistant paint. (Don't do any painting unless your conure is out of the room.) Cleaning up splatters and dried foods is much easier if you have a durable, washable wall.

10. Keep a container of antibacterial liquid soap handy. You can use a squirt or two in the soft foods and water cups for easy cleaning. Scrub hot, soapy water around in the cups, being careful to get every bit of debris or slime out of the cups. Then rinse well until all traces of soap and soap scent are gone. Fill as usual, and replace in the cage.

Chapter Seven

Living with Conures

Living with a conure can be very much like living with a small child—children are curious, energetic, loud, and into everything! Given the opportunity, conures will behave the same way. These little parrots are so intelligent that you need to be prepared to keep them entertained, mentally stimulated, and busy. If left unchallenged, they can become bored and depressed. Some bored conures develop bad habits such as screaming, biting, feather plucking, or self-mutilation.

A conure that spends a great deal of time inside the cage must be provided with stimulating, interesting toys, a great diet, and plenty of safe things to chew. Fun times spent outside the cage must be constantly supervised. Busy conures simply have to poke their beaks into everything they see, and they must be watched every minute to make sure they don't get themselves into dangerous situations.

Topping the list of in-home dangers for pet birds of all types is the

Keep your conure away from leaded or ornamental items that might contain harmful materials.

risk of drowning. Open toilets, uncovered aquariums, hot tubs, even partially filled vases or drinking glasses pose drowning hazards. Other dangers include being crushed by sleeping humans, accidents with other pets, poisoning, and the possibility of being injured in unsafe cages. See why you have to stay one step ahead of your conure at all times?

Conure-Proofing Your Home

Homes with conures must be conure-proofed in much the same way that homes with small children are child-proofed. Take a look around your home and see how many dangers are waiting for curious beaks to pry into them. Are there uncovered electrical outlets? Are wires and cables from appliances and computers out of reach of interested beaks? Are cleaning solutions or chemicals left out or uncovered? Many things in our homes that present no danger to us can be life-threatening to a curious

Busy Gold-cap.

conure. Take a few minutes to check each room of your home for items that may be unsafe. Some rooms of your home will be more dangerous than others, so be on the lookout for potential hazards. Here are some things to watch for:

• *Exposed electrical outlets and cords.* All electrical outlets within reach of your conure should be capped or covered. Your local hardware store carries items specifically made for this use, and you should purchase enough to take care of every conure-accessible outlet in your home. Any wiring, cords, or cables must be tucked out of sight or otherwise be made impossible to reach. A conure's sharp hookbill can slice through electric cords or telephone lines in a split second. To avoid the chance of an electrical shock or burn to your conure, make sure it can never get its beak on these items.

• *Water.* Aquariums, toilets, indoor ponds, hot tubs, any containers of water or other fluids, vases, or drinking glasses containing even tiny amounts of liquid must be covered or removed whenever your conure is out of its cage. Birds have been known to tip over and fall into cups or glasses and drown. And since most conures enjoy splashing around in water, they might attempt to play or bathe in any water they find. Toilets are especially dangerous because they are impossible for a daring conure to climb out of. Your beautiful aquarium also poses several risks. Fascinated by the colorful, moving fish, an interested conure may try to lean into a tank to get a closer look and fall in. Or it may try to bathe in the tank and be unable to climb back out. Don't take any risks. Cover, remove, or empty all containers of water whenever your conure is playing outside the safety of its cage.

• *Ceiling fans.* Ceiling fans pose a potentially fatal danger. They should be turned off whenever your conure is outside the cage. Even with clipped wings, many conures will take flight if startled and could fly into the rotating blades. To crash into a whirling ceiling fan would mean certain injury or death. If you have ceiling fans in your home, make sure that your conure is confined to its cage during operation, and turn them off whenever your conure is playing outside the cage.

There are devices made to shield the fan blades from pet birds. Ask at your local hardware store for details.

• *Windows*. Make sure all windows are screened or closed when your conure is outside its cage, especially if your conure is flighted. It is also a good idea to keep curtains or sheers pulled together to avoid crashes into the glass. Other dangers include the possibility of an attack by a cat or dog that has sneaked in through an unscreened window. And there's yet another danger to think about: Your conure might escape! Escapes occur far too frequently, and can have tragic consequences for pet conures.

• *Doors*. Some conures like to perch on the tops of open doors. This habit could result in crushing injuries should the door be slammed shut. Or the conure could be killed or hurt should it try to follow someone through a door and be caught in the door as it closes. The key to avoiding these types of injuries is to always know where your conure is every second it's outside the cage. Also keep an eye out for any dog or cat that may sneak in through an open door. Conures have been attacked by animals that have quietly come in without being noticed. And don't forget the possibility that your conure may zoom out an open door and away!

• *Mirrors*. Sometimes a conure might not realize that mirrors are solid surfaces and will try to fly through them. This could result in broken bones, concussions, or even worse, in death. If your conure is flighted, consider adding decals to mirrors, or covering them when your conure is outside the cage.

• *Cushions and blankets*. Some conures enjoy burrowing and may nestle down behind, or under, throw pillows. If your conure likes to hide in blankets or take naps under covers, it could be fatally injured when someone unknowingly sits down on it. If you plan to allow your conure to play on the furniture, make sure everyone knows when it is out so as to avoid accidental injuries. And while it may be tempting to take a nap with your conure, never, *ever* sleep with it! Many conures have died when their owners rolled over on them in their sleep, resulting in the suffocation or crushing death of the conures. The safest place for your conure to sleep is inside its cage.

• *Young children*. Not realizing how fragile birds are, a child might handle your conure too roughly. A very

Remove or empty any containers of liquid that might tempt your conure.

Always supervise interactions between your conure and children.

young child might not understand that a brightly colored conure is much different from a toy and could squeeze, crush, or step on it. Also, a nervous conure might nip a child, causing the youngster to retaliate by slapping or hitting it. It would be a good idea to put your conure in a locked or safe room off limits to visiting children. While an older child is more likely to safely handle a conure, make sure you are there to supervise any and all interaction. You can never be too careful.

• *Ashtrays.* Clean or remove from reach any ashtrays containing cigarette butts. The filter tips will be loaded with nicotine, and eating one or two could kill your conure! Better yet, smoke outside—or quit.

• *Scented candles and potpourri.* Anything that has a strong smell can be hazardous to conures. The avian respiratory system is much more sensitive than that of humans, and can be harmed by the various essential oils, perfumes, or chemicals used to scent these items. If you have these things in your home, use them only in rooms that are off limits to your conure, and make sure that the rooms are well ventilated. There is also the danger that your conure might sneak a nibble of candle wax or eat a few pieces of that pretty potpourri. To be safe, don't allow your conure to have access to candles or potpourri—or better yet, don't use them.

• *Cleaners and chemicals.* Air fresheners, aerosol sprays, deodorizers, detergents, drain cleaners, fabric softeners, furniture polishes, glues, hairspray, incense, mineral spirits, mothballs, nail polish and remover, nicotine patches or gum, oven cleaners, over-the-counter medications, pain relievers, perfumes, prescription medications, shoe polish, soaps and shampoos, and window cleaners are all things commonly found in the home that can be deadly to conures. Make sure to tightly close and put away any of these items when you have finished with them. It wouldn't take much of these toxins to kill your precious conure.

• *Insect poisons*. Due to the low body weights of conures, even tiny bits of ingested poisons such as insecticides, pesticides, and herbicides can kill them. If your dog or cat wears a flea collar, keep the animal away from your conure to avoid exposing it to the chemicals. Ask your veterinarian to recommend a safe alternative. If you need to spray or treat your home with an insecticide, take your conure to a safe location outside the home, such as a neighbor's house. Don't bring your conure back until at least 24 hours have passed, and all fumes and odors have dissipated. Be sure to vacuum the carpets and wipe down all surfaces your conure may come in contact with before allowing it to play outside the cage.

• *Heavy metals*. Check your home for any items that may contain lead, cadmium, mercury, copper, or zinc. Batteries, fishing lures, lead crystal, leaded lamps, stained glass items, drapery weights, some bird toy weights, jewelry, solder, some paints, thermometers, shampoo (especially dandruff preparations), some older miniblinds, and many other items contain heavy metal compounds. If you are in doubt about a product, carefully read the label. If it contains heavy metals, keep it away from your conure. In most cases, only a small amount ingested by a chewing conure could be enough to kill it. Too many conures and other pet birds have died after gnawing on decorative leaded lamps or stained glass objects.

• *Carbon monoxide*. Carbon monoxide is a colorless, odorless, and tasteless gas that may be produced as the result of an imperfect or incomplete combustion of fuel. Should they malfunction, some home appliances such as gas dryers, furnaces, or water heaters may emit carbon monoxide fumes. Other possible sources of carbon monoxide fumes are wood burning, coal, or kerosene heaters, and gas stoves. To prevent accidents with any of these items, have a professional check them periodically to make sure everything is functioning as it should. As long as these appliances are in good working condition, there should be no danger to your conure or to your family. Auto exhaust fumes are also rich in carbon monoxide. Never keep your conure in a garage, or in a location where vehicle exhaust can reach it. These fumes not only contain carbon dioxide, but other toxic gases and can be deadly to your conure. You might consider investing in a carbon

PTFE Fumes

Polytetraflouethylene (PTFE) fumes are airborne and can penetrate other rooms in the house outside of the kitchen, even rooms upstairs or located several doors away from the kitchen. Nonstick cookware was once thought to be dangerous only when overheated, but has shown to be potentially dangerous even when used at normal temperatures. Heating the pans or other coated items causes a breakdown in PTFE, which creates the deadly fumes. In a best-case scenario, the only problem would be that your conure would be uncomfortable, but unfortunately, too many conures and other pet birds have died from these fumes to make that scenario acceptable.

What happens when a conure breathes PTFE fumes? The colorless fumes affect the conure's delicate respiratory system, and causes severe distress and all too often, a painful death. Many pet birds have been found dead for seemingly unknown causes, only to have it determined that they died from exposure to PTFE fumes. And even though a conure may not seem to be affected at the time, problems can develop later.

If you must use nonstick cookware, open a window in the kitchen while cooking, never overheat the pans, and try to put as many rooms between your conure and the kitchen as possible. Close all the doors, and make sure the room your conure is in is well ventilated. Carefully monitor your conure for any breathing distress. If you think your conure has been exposed to PTFE fumes, immediately open a window or take the conure outside so it can breathe fresh air. Telephone your avian veterinarian if you think a visit to the doctor might be in order. To be safe, don't use nonstick cookware at all! Cast iron is a good choice, as are stainless steel pots and pans.

monoxide monitor for your home. This will help protect both your family and your conure.

• *Polytetraflouethylene fumes.* Nonstick cookware and other items coated with the chemical polytetraflouethylene present a serious and deadly danger. This chemical is found in self-cleaning ovens, griddles, baking sheets, muffin pans, irons and ironing board covers, cooking utensils, curling irons, oven baking bags, certain types of lightbulbs, and other commonly used items in the home. For the safety of your conure, consider using only stainless steel pots and pans, ventilate rooms when the oven or other items coated with PTFE are used, and avoid using the self-cleaning feature of your oven to cut down the risk of deadly fumes.

Conure-Safe Cleaning and Disinfecting

Because a conure's respiratory system is so sensitive, strong household cleaners should never be used around it. If you can smell the cleaners, they're probably bad for your conure. Conures have died from inhaling fumes even when they were in rooms considered to be a safe distance from the items in question. And not only can the fumes from these products cause your own eyes to water and your sinuses to burn, they can be deadly to your conure.

If you have to use such cleaners, remove your conure to a well-ventilated area of the home, preferably in a room with a door you can close. Vent the area you are cleaning by opening a window and don't bring your conure back into the room until all the fumes have dissipated. Some items to avoid are carpet cleaners and deodorizers, bleach, toilet cleaners and granular sink cleaners, drain cleaners, ammonia-based cleaners, window and glass cleaners, and any other harsh cleansers. Keep all items out of reach of your conure so it won't have a chance to sneak a taste of any chemicals, or breathe any fumes.

To clean up conure messes, a vinegar and water solution is handy for wiping down grimy cage bars and scrubbing off the droppings. Rinse well afterward with lots of fresh water. A mild bleach and water solution also can be used to scrub down and disinfect dirty cages. Rinse well after using the solution. If you can still smell any bleach odor after rinsing, continue rinsing until all the smell is gone before you put your conure back into the cage.

Check your pet or bird store for packaged cage cleaning preparations that are safe for use around conures. These solutions clean sticky or hard, dried-on messes without damaging the finish on your conure's cage. Always follow the instructions on the package.

Toxic Plants

Did you know that many common houseplants, flowers, and trees are deadly to conures? If you have live plants of any kind in your home, you need to know whether or not they are conure-safe. Unfortunately, it can be difficult to know which ones are safe and which are toxic. And because even safe items can be harmful if your conure consumes a large amount of a particular plant, a good general rule is to restrict your conure's access to all houseplants and trees in your home.

Houseplants

You may run across different lists containing the names of plants and trees that are considered to be dangerous (or safe) for conures. It's possible to find some plants noted as dangerous in one list, while another list may name the same plants to be safe! If you have any questions about the safety of a particular plant for your conure, be sure to discuss your concerns with your avian veterinarian.

Following is a listing of plants and trees considered to be dangerous to conures. Notice that not all parts of each plant on the list are toxic. In some cases the ripened fruit is safe, while the branches, sap, unripe fruit, seeds or pits, or foliage are toxic. The list is by no means complete; because there are so many, many plants and trees, some items may have been missed. If you aren't sure what species of plant you have in your home or yard, consult a nursery to verify the identities. Sometimes, plant names vary by region.

- **Acokanthera** (*Acokanthera* species)
- **Amaryllis** (*Amaryllis* species)
- **Angel's Trumpet** (*Datura* species)
- **Apricot** (*Prunus armeniaca*)
- **Apple** (*Malus* species). The fruit is safe; avoid seeds.
- **Avocado** (*Persea americaca*)
- **Azalea** (*Rhododendron canadensis*)
- **Balsam Pear** (*Memordica charanita*)
- **Baneberry** (*Actaea rubra, A. pachypoda*)
- **Bird of Paradise** (*Poinciana gilliensii*)
- **Bittersweet** (*Celastrus* species)
- **Black Locust** (*Robinia pseudo-acacia*)
- **Boxwood** (*Buxus* species)
- **Bracken Fern** (*Pteridium aquilinium*)
- **Buckthorn** (*Karwinskia humboldtiana* and related species)
- **Burdock** (*Arctium* species)
- **Buttercup** (*Ranunculus* species)
- **Caladium** (*Caladium* species)
- **Calla Lily** (*Zantedeschia aethiopica*)
- **Catclaw Acacia** (*Acacia greggii*)
- **Caster Bean** (*Ricinus communis*)
- **Cherry** (*Prunus* species)
- **Chinaberry** (*Melia azadarach*)
- **Clematis** (*Clematis montana* and related species)
- **Coral Plant** (*Jatropha mutifida*)
- **Crocus** (*Cholchicum autumnale*)
- **Cyad** or **Sago Cyas** (*Cyas revoluta*)
- **Daffodil** (*Narcissus* species)
- **Daphne** (*Daphne* species)
- **Delphinium** (*Delphinium* species)
- **Devil's Ivy** (*Epipremnum aureum*)
- **Dieffenbachia, dumb cane** (*Dieffenbachia* species)
- **Eggplant** (*Solanum melongena*)
- **Elderberry** (*Sambucus mexicana*)
- **Elephant's Ear** (*Colocasia* species)
- **Euonymus** (*Euonymus* species)
- **Figs** (*Ficus* species)
- **Four o'clock** (*Miribilis jalapa*)
- **Foxglove** (*Digitalis purpurea*)
- **Heliotrope** (*Heliotropium* species)
- **Henbane** (*Hyoscyamus niger*)
- **Holly** (*Hex aquifolium*)
- **Horse Chestnut** (*Aesculus hippocastanum* and related species)
- **Horse Nettle** (*Solanum carolinense*)
- **Hyacinth** (*Hyacinthus orietalis*)
- **Hydrangea** (*Hydrangea* species)
- **Iris** (*Iris* species)
- **Ivy** (*Hedera* species)

- **Jack-in-the-Pulpit** (*Arisaema* species)
- **Jerusalem Cherry** (*Solanum pseudocapsicum*)
- **Jessamine, Yellow** (*Gelsemium sempervirens*)
- **Jimsonweed** (*Datura* species)
- **Jonquil** (*Narcissus jonquilla*)
- **Juniper** (*Juniperus* species)
- **Lantana** (*Lantana camara*)
- **Larkspur** (*Delphinium* species)
- **Laurel** (*Kalmia* species)
- **Lily-of-the-Valley** (*Convalleria majalis*)
- **Lobelia** (*Lobelia* species)
- **Locoweed** (*Astragalus* species, *Oxytrophis* species)
- **Lupine** (*Lupinus* species)
- **Mistletoe** (*Santalales*). Avoid the berries.
- **Mock Orange** (*Philadelphus* species)
- **Moonseed** (*Menispermum canadense*)
- **Monkshood** (*Aconitum* species)
- **Morning Glory** (*Ipomoea violacea*)
- **Mushrooms** (*Amanita* species, others)
- **Narcissus** (*Narcissus* species)
- **Oleander** (*Nerium oleander*)
- **Peach** (*Prunus persica*). The fruit is safe.
- **Pear** (*Pyrus* species). The fruit is safe.
- **Peony** (*Paeonia officinalis*)
- **Periwinkle** (*Vinca minor, Vinca rosea*)
- **Peyote** (*Lophophora williamsii*)
- **Philodendron** (*Philodendron* species)
- **Plum** (*Prunus* species)
- **Poison Hemlock** (*Conium maculatum*)
- **Poison Ivy** (*Toxicodendron radicans*)
- **Poison Oak** (*Toxicodendron quercifolium, T. diversilobum*)
- **Poison Sumac** (*Rhux vernix*)
- **Poinsettia** (*Euphorbia pulcherrima*)
- **Poppy** (*Papaver somniferum*)
- **Pokeweed** (*Phytolacca americana*)
- **Potato** (*Solanum tuberosum*)
- **Pothos** (*Eprimemnun aureum*)
- **Primrose** (*Primula* species)
- **Privet** (*Ligustrum vulgare*)
- **Ragwort** (*Senecio jacobea*)
- **Rhododendron** (*Rhododendron* species)
- **Rhubarb** (*Rheum rhapoticum*)
- **Rosary Pea** (*Abrus precatorius*)
- **Sage** (*Salvia officinalis*)
- **Shamrock Plant** (*Medicago lupulina*)
- **Snowdrop** (*Galanthus nivalis*)
- **Sorrel** (*Rumex* species)
- **Star of Bethlehem** (*Ornithogalum umbellatum*)
- **Sweet Pea** (*Lathyrus latifolius*)
- **Tobacco** (*Nicotiania* species)
- **Tulip** (*Tulipa* species)
- **Virginia Creeper** (*Panthenocissus quinquefolia*)
- **Vetches** (*Vicia* species)
- **Water Hemlock** (*Cicuta maculata*)
- **Waxberry** (*Symphoricarpos albus*)
- **Western Yew** (*Taxus breviflora*)
- **Wisteria** (*Wisteria* species)

Remember, there may be other toxic plants not included in this list. To be on the safe side, restrict your conure's access to any plants or potted trees in your home unless you are absolutely sure the item is safe. If you have any doubts, consult your veterinarian.

Safe Plants

Many plants and trees are considered to be beneficial for conures, but remember that any item (leaves, fruits, berries) can be harmful if ingested in too large a quantity. The following items are thought to be safe for conures, but if you have any doubts, consult your avian veterinarian or call your local plant nursery.

- **Abelia** (*Abelia* species)
- **Acacia** (*Acacia* species)
- **African Daisy** (*Arctotis stoechadifolia*)
- **African Violet** (*Saintpaulina* species)
- **Aluminum Plant** (*Pilea cadierei*)
- **Aloe** (*Aloe* species). The flesh only.
- **Aralis** (*Aralia* species)
- **Arbutus** (*Arbutus* species)
- **Areca, Butterfly Cane** (*Areca lutescens*)
- **Ash** (*Fraxinus* species)
- **Asparagus Fern** (*Asparagus densiflorus*)
- **Aspen** (*Populus* species)
- **Aspidistra** (*Aspidistra* species)
- **Baby's Tears** (*Helix soleirolli*)
- **Baby's Breath** (*Gypsophila paniculata*)
- **Bachelor Buttons** (*Centauria cyanus*)
- **Barberry** (*Berberis* species)
- **Beech** (*Fagus*, *Nothofagus*)
- **Begonia** (*Begonis* species)
- **Birch** (*Betula* species)
- **Bird's Nest Fern** (*Asplenium nidus*)
- **Blood Leaf Plant** (*Iresine herbstii*)
- **Boston Fern** (*Nephrolepsis bostoniensis*)
- **Bougainvillea** (*Bougainvillea* species)
- **Bromeliads** (*Anans comosus*)
- **California Holly** (*Herteromeles arbutifolia*)
- **Calamint** (*Calamint* species)
- **Calendula, Pot Marigold** (*Calendula offincinalis*)
- **Camellia** (*Camellis* species)
- **Chamomile** (*Chamaemelum nobile*)
- **Chickweed** (*Cerastium vulgatum, Stellaria media*)
- **Chicory** (*Cichorium intybus*)
- **Cissus Kangaroo Vines** (*Cissus* species)
- **Claw Cactus** (*Schlumbergera truncata*)
- **Coffee Tree** (*Coffea arabica*). Avoid feeding coffee.
- **Coleus** (*Coleus blumei*)
- **Comfrey** (*Symphytum officinalis*)
- **Corn Plant** (*Dracaena fragrans*)
- **Cottonwood** (*Populus* species)
- **Crabapple** (*Malus* species). Fruit is safe.
- **Creeping Jenny** (*Lysimachia* species)
- **Croton** (*Codiaeum variegatum*)
- **Dahlia** (*Dahlia* species)
- **Dandelion** (*Taraxacum officinalis*)
- **Date** (*Phoenix dactylifera*)
- **Daylily** (*Hermerocallis* species)
- **Dill** (*Anethum graveolen*)
- **Dogwood** (*Cornus* species)
- **Donkey Tail** (*Sedum morganianum*)
- **Dracaena** (*Dracaena* species)
- **Dragon Tree** (*Dracaena draco*)
- **Easter Cactus** (*Rhipsalidopsis* species)
- **Elm** (*Ulmus* species)
- **European Fan** (*Chamaerops humilis*)

- **Echeveria** (*Echeveria* species)
- **Elephant Foot Tree** (*Beaucarnea recurvata*)
- **Eucalyptus** (*Eucalyptus* species)
- **Eugenia** (*Eugenia* species)
- **Fir** (*Abies* species)
- **Gold Dust Dracaena** (*Dracaena godseffiana*)
- **Gardenia** (*Gardenia jasminoides*)
- **Garlic** (*Allium sativum*)
- **Gloxinia** (*Sinningia speciosa*)
- **Grape Ivy** (*Cissus rhombifolia*)
- **Grape Vine** (*Vitis* species)
- **Hens and Chicks** (*Echeveria, Sempervivum* species)
- **Hibiscus** (*Hibiscus rosa-sinensis*)
- **Honeysuckle** (*Lonicera* species)
- **Hoya** (*Hoya* species)
- **Impatiens** (*Impatiens* species)
- **Indian Hawthorne** (*Rhaphiolepsis* species)
- **Jade Plant** (*Crassula ovata*)
- **Kalanchoe** (*Kalanchoe blossfeldiana*)
- **Larch** (*Larix* species)
- **Lemon Balm** (*Melissa officinalis*)
- **Lilac** (*Syringa vulgaris*)
- **Lily, Easter** or **Tiger** (*Lilium* species)
- **Magnolia** (*Magnolia* species)
- **Marigold** (*Tagetes* species)
- **Maidenhair Fern** (*Adiantum* species)
- **Manzanita** (*Arctostapylos manzanita*)
- **Mayapple** (*Podophyllum peltatum*). Fruit only.
- **Monkey Plant** (*Ruellia* species)
- **Moses-in-the-Cradle** (*Rhoeo spathacea*)
- **Mother-in-Law's-Tongue** (*Sansevieria trifasciata*)
- **Nandina** (*Nandina domestica*)
- **Nasturtium** (*Tropaeolum majus*)
- **Natal Plum** (*Carissa macrocarpa*)
- **Nerve Plant** (*Fittonia verschaffeltti*)
- **Norfolk Island Pine** (*Araucaria excelsa*)
- **Passionflower** (*Passiflora caerulea*)
- **Peppermint** (*Mentha x piperita*)
- **Peperomia** (*Peperomia* species)
- **Petunia** (*Petunia* species)
- **Ponytail Plant** (*Beaucarnea recurvata*)
- **Prayer Plant** (*Maranta leuconeura*)
- **Purple Passion, Purple Velvet** (*Gynura aurantiaca*)
- **Pyracantha** (*Pyracantha* species)
- **Raphiolepis** (*Raphiolepis* species)
- **Rose** (*Rosa* species)
- **Rubber Plant** (*Ficus elastica*)
- **Russian Olive** (*Elaeagnus augustifolia*)
- **Schefflera** (*Schefflera actinophylla*)
- **Sensitive Plant** (*Mimosa pudica*)
- **Spearmint** (*Mentha spicata*)
- **Spider Plant** (*Chlorophytum comosum*)
- **Spruce** (*Picea* species)
- **Squirrel's Foot Fern** (*Davallia trichomanoides*)
- **Staghorn, Elk's Horn** (*Platycerium bifurcatum*)
- **Star Jasmine** (*Trachelospermum jasminoides*)
- **String of Beads** (*Senecio rowleyanus*)
- **Swedish Ivy** (*Plectranthus australis*)
- **Sword Fern** (*Nephrolepis exaltata*)
- **Thistle** (*Cirsium* species)
- **Ti Plant** (*Cordyline terminalis*)
- **Violet** (*Viola* species)
- **Wandering Jew** (*Tradescantia fluminensis*)
- **Willow** (*Salix* species)
- **Yucca** (*Yucca* species)
- **Zebra Plant** (*Aphelandra squarrosa*)

Other Dangers in the Home

Pets

Conures simply don't realize how little they are and this attitude often gets them into trouble with other pets. A tiny conure may think nothing of challenging a much larger bird for its territory, of chasing the family dog away from its own food dish, or of taking a bath in the cat's water bowl. You have to keep an eye on each and every encounter between your conure and other pets. It takes only a split second for something terrible and irreversible to happen.

Even though your other pets may have been tolerant of your conure before, there's no guarantee that they will stay that way. They may feel threatened or jealous of your conure, and might also be territorial. When your conure is playing on the floor, remember that it is on what may be considered personal property by your cat or dog. You might consider putting away the dog or cat toys so the conure can't play with them and stir up defensive behavior on the part of the furred members of the family. It is also a good idea to make sure that your conure isn't picking on the cat or dog!

Is Your Conure Safe Inside Its Cage?

If you have other pets, make sure you know where they are at all times. Even though your conure may be locked inside its cage, a cat might be able to reach a paw through the bars and maul it. Or a dog could tip over the cage and allow your conure to escape. Either way, your feathered friend could be killed or seriously injured.

Dog and Cat Toxins

It takes only a tiny bit of saliva from the mouth of a cat or dog to make a conure sick—the E. coli can be passed to your conure from any mammal. If your conure is ever injured by a cat or dog, don't waste time. Rush it to an avian veterinarian as soon as possible. Even what appears to be a minor scratch could be deadly, and the first hours after an injury are critical. Cats carry the pasteurella bacteria, and this bacteria is so toxic that even a tiny bit from a scratch can kill a conure unless an

Negligence Equals Disaster

One cockatiel owner thought she had securely closed the door behind her when she walked from one room to the next, but the door didn't catch. It swung open and the family's cat slipped into the room. By the time the owner heard the commotion, the cat had poked its paw between the cage bars and clawed the defenseless bird inside. Though the cockatiel survived the initial attack, the toxins in the cat's claws had entered the bird's system. Sadly, it died the next day.

Iguanas may infect your conure with salmonella.

antitoxin is injected immediately. Unfortunately, even after receiving the antitoxin, many birds die.

Even though your animals may have been gentle with your conure in the past, you never know when they may decide to bite or claw it without warning. In some cases, conures have survived attacks from cats or dogs, but it's not worth the danger to take chances. Closely monitor all interactions between your conure and your cats or dogs.

Other Pets in the Home

Reptiles, rodents, and conures don't mix! Keep your conure away from the cages of any other types of pets. Conures have lost toes or received severe bites when climbing on another pet's cage. There are also dangerous bacteria and toxins present in the saliva of some reptiles that can harm your conure, and their droppings could make your conure sick should it eat any of them. Some

lizards, iguanas, and snakes are known to carry salmonella.

Reptiles or even very tame ferrets or rats may attack your conure. Be safe and let your conure admire your other pets from a distance.

Helpful hint: After handling other pets such as these, avoid spreading germs or bacteria from one pet to another by always washing your hands and changing your clothes before handling your conure.

Other Birds

Territorial parrots can severely injure or kill a curious conure. Amazon parrots, cockatoos, African greys, and macaws can deliver major bites, clip off toes, or even rip off a smaller bird's beak. As if that wasn't bad enough, there have been times when jealous birds have fought and injured each other over spending time with a favorite person. Some squabbles aren't too serious, but if things begin to get out of hand,

Even parrots that have previously gotten along may squabble, so supervise all interactions. Green-cheeked conure and Senegal parrot.

make sure you're right there to intervene. Never let your birds play together without supervision. Even conures of the same species don't always get along.

Playing on the Floor

Be sure everybody knows the conure is out if it likes to run around on the floor. Playing on the floor can be a lot of fun, but sadly, many conures have died after being accidentally stepped on. If you want to let your conure play on the floor, put its toys in a clear area that is out of the main path through your home, and constantly supervise its activities. Conures can be quick, so be ready to

head it off at the pass if it makes a dash toward a danger zone. Also, a conure on the floor is easy prey for curious or territorial cats and dogs, so be prepared to step in before anybody gets nipped or scratched. If you can't watch your conure every second when it's playing on the floor, return it to the safety of its cage.

Dangers Outside the Home

Never carry your conure outside on your shoulder. A gust of wind might be all that is needed to carry it away into the treetops. Loud noises or other distractions could startle your conure and it might very easily take flight, even if its wings are clipped. Escaped birds are sometimes recaptured, but all too often they are never seen again. Don't take that chance. If you want to take your conure outside, confine it to a safe carrier or inside a cage with secure locks that won't come open if the cage gets bumped.

Escapes

What if your conure escapes? Do you have any hope of getting it back? The answer is a cautious yes; many escaped birds have been successfully recovered. If your conure escapes, try these things to maximize your chances of recovery:

• Set your conure's familiar cage outside where it can be easily seen by the escapee, and leave the door open. Fill the cups with some of your conure's favorite foods and clean water to tempt it to return when it gets hungry or thirsty.

• Stay in the area where you last saw your conure, and continue to call for it. Don't give up too soon. Your conure may not have gone too far away, and might respond to your voice.

• Post flyers featuring color pictures of your conure along with a written description in bold lettering beneath the photo. Don't forget to include pertinent contact information.

• Call neighbors and let them know your conure is on the loose, and ask them to keep an eye out for it.

• Put ads in the newspaper, and call up local broadcasting stations and ask them to mention your lost conure.

• Notify local police stations, veterinarians, pet stores, and animal shelters.

Whatever you decide to do, don't give up. Take encouragement from the fact that some lost conures have been successfully recovered.

Predators

A conure sitting unprotected on top of a perch or playstand is fair game for predators such as hawks, snakes, raccoons, or other wild animals. There is also the risk of disease transmission from wild birds or other wildlife. Don't put your conure in danger. Keep it inside a cage or carrier, and never leave it outside unattended!

Always protect your conure when you take it outside.

Flint and the Dog

Flint, a big bold Patagonian conure, enjoyed frequent outings in the yard with her family. While she romped on the grass, the family sat around her in a circle, laughing at her antics. One day, as Flint playfully scampered from person to person, a neighbor's dog rushed into the yard and stuck its nose down to sniff the parrot. Flint bit the dog's toe. Before anyone could move, the dog snapped its jaws, and the beautiful Patagonian conure was killed instantly.

Outdoor Pets

Outdoor pets also can be danger-ous threats to conures. Unfamiliar with the feathered creature in the cage or sitting loose on your shoul-der, a dog or cat might attack. Or the conure could flutter onto the ani-mal, causing it to panic. The reaction would be too rapid for you to be able to stop, and your conure could be seriously injured or killed.

Toys, Toys, Toys

As discussed on pages 89–90, every conure needs a selection of good-quality, bird-safe toys. You can pick these up in any pet store, and lots of department stores have selections of bird toys, too. Don't forget to shop the dog toy section; many dog toys make great toys for conures, and can be cheaper than the ones in the bird aisle. There are also many fine Internet sites and magazines that feature bird toys.

When choosing toys for your conure, carefully check the materials used as well as the construction of the toy. It should be made of safe materials that contain no lead, harm-ful paints, or chemical dyes. Avoid toys made of fragile material, such as brittle plastic that could harm your conure. Cotton rope toys are great fun, but should be checked fre-quently for frayed threads that might wrap around a toe. These items can be machine washed when soiled.

Discard any leather or rawhide toys that wind up in the water cup, because they can't be sterilized once they've been soaked.

Note: Always make sure that leather or rawhide is not tanned or treated with chemicals. You can buy untreated leather at many pet or bird stores. Ask the manager if you're uncertain whether the leather toy you're interested in is untreated. Some stores even sell leather strips and chunks of bird-safe wood that you can buy for making your own conure toys.

When shopping for toys, remem-ber that conures have strong beaks and should be given only toys meant for medium-sized to large-sized par-rots. Tiny toys meant for parakeets or other small birds are much too fragile for conures.

Homemade Fun

There are plenty of things lying around your home that will make fine playthings for your conure. Toi-let tissue and paper towel rolls, small cardboard boxes, junk mail, post-cards, and other tough paper arti-cles are fun for your conure to shred. Make sure to remove any staples or glue from paper items before turning them over to your conure, and supervise any play involving paper tubes. Some adventurous conures have gotten their heads stuck.

Other "free" toys are the hard plastic tops to soda bottles, wooden spools, popsicle sticks, empty facial tissue boxes, paper bags, wooden mixing spoons, and short strips of clean fabric tied in knots. Some conures enjoy climbing inside small paper bags and pulling the open ends down. Making paper bag "tents" can be lots of fun for conures!

Dangerous Items

Keep rubber bands, small plastic beads, fragile glass ornaments, any items containing lead such as fishing weights, old jewelry or stained glass, paper clips, tacks, straight pins, safety pins, small marbles, and painted or shellacked wooden items out of reach. Also avoid leaving permanent markers or correction fluids open because the fumes from these items can make your conure ill. Keys and key rings pose other potential dangers—your conure's tongue could get caught in the key ring, and chewing on the keys might result in metal toxicity.

Be vigilant when putting things away and don't leave anything unsafe where your conure can find it. Remember, as mentioned earlier, these smart little parrots are a lot like children. Everything they pick up goes into their mouths!

Replace rope toys when they become frayed.

Chapter Eight

Conure Behavior and Training

Conures are famous for their bizarre behavior. Comical and affectionate, these little parrots can be bossy, demanding, stubborn, and opinionated. Pet conures would rule the household if given the chance. Some of their favorite activities include tugging at the fingers of their human companions to encourage head scratches and caresses, snuggling up with toys for naps, hiding under the cage liner, or trying to steal tastes of whatever food they see the humans of the household eating.

These smart birds can learn to do simple tricks, such as shaking hands, waving good-bye, or emptying and refilling a small toy box. They even show preference over which foot they use for holding food and toys! Watch your conure to see if it is a righty or a lefty. And don't be surprised to see it reach a foot down into a cup of food, feel around until it has a "handful," then nibble whatever it brings up.

Uncontrolled screaming can become a big problem!

A conure's body language is very similar to that of other parrots, but since each conure's personality is distinctly different, what means one thing for one conure could mean something entirely different for your conure. Pay attention to your conure's daily activities and you will see that it demonstrates certain behaviors in response to certain things. Below are some of the things you will probably see your conure do.

Twenty Common Conure Behaviors

1. *Crouching slightly on the perch, leaning forward, wings quivering.* Don't be alarmed if your conure does this, even though it can appear that it is in distress. It isn't sick or hurt; it just wants to be picked up, petted, given a treat, or have you pay attention to it in some way. Some conures can appear to be quite desperate!

2. *Perched steadily on one foot, fluffed slightly, eyes closed.* A healthy conure displaying this posture is sleepy or napping.

3. *Pupils contracting and expanding (referred to as pinning, pinpointing, or flashing); head feathers squared; body feathers tight, possibly growling or hissing.* Don't get too close if your conure is doing this. These actions signify aggression, and a conure behaving in this manner will probably bite anyone it can reach.

4. *Tight body feathers, clinging to cage bars; sitting very tall, possibly trembling.* This behavior signifies fear or nervousness. Soothe your conure with soft words and, if it will allow it, stroke it gently. Try to find out what frightened your conure and do what you can to alleviate the situation. Reassure your conure that it is safe.

5. *Holding up one foot when approached.* Many tame conures will do this when they want to be picked up.

6. *Turning the head from side to side, staring at something with one*

Some conures love to snuggle!

eye. A conure doing this is displaying curiosity and interest. You might also notice this behavior when teaching your conure to talk. An interested conure might focus on your mouth, tilt its head, and listen intently.

7. *Striking or slashing, beak open.* Conures can and will bite, sometimes severely. If your conure is striking at you, stay out of reach! Those sharp hookbills can easily rip through the skin. Find out why your conure is behaving aggressively, and attempt to relieve the situation. If another pet, person, or bird is upsetting your conure, remove them from the area. Remember, don't try to touch your conure when it is acting this way. You could put yourself in danger of receiving a painful bite.

8. *Head bobbing or weaving; rhythmic swaying back and forth; wing movement.* Conures love music, and will often respond to the rhythms by doing a conure version of dancing. These actions are usually associated with playfulness; however, since conure personalities vary so much from bird to bird, this behavior may also signify aggression. Very young birds will bob their heads to beg for food. Learn to distinguish between playfulness, begging, and aggression by studying your conure's daily behavior.

9. *Tilting the head down, fluffing the feathers and closing the eyes; slowly scratching the neck or head with a toe.* A conure behaving in this manner is petting itself. You might also see it using a dropped feather or small toy to scratch its neck or head. Your conure is inviting you to pet it, so join in the game by gently touching its head or feathers.

10. *Rapid head bobbing; regurgitation; feeding a favorite person or toy.* This action signifies affection or love, and can be sexual behavior. Regurgitation is not to be confused with vomiting, which is a sign of illness and should be checked out by a veterinarian.

11. *Tongue touching.* A conure's tongue is extremely sensitive, and a curious conure will often probe something with its tongue to feel the object. An affectionate conure might kiss you by pressing its tongue against your skin.

12. *Panting, with beak open, wings held away from the body, tight feathers.* This means that your conure is overheated and is trying to cool down. If your conure's cage is directly in front of a window, either shade the window or move the cage away. Sunlight coming in full force can cause a conure to overheat in no time. Cool the room, and perhaps mist the conure with water.

13. *Backing up to or rubbing against an object or a favorite person's hand.* A conure doing this is masturbating. Many will choose an item in the cage or a special toy as a surrogate mate. If the behavior becomes obsessive, offer distractions such as a new toy or game, or remove the item the conure is fixated on. If you are the object of affection, don't overreact and don't encourage the behavior.

A Nanday conure asking to be picked up.

14. *Beak grinding.* If you notice your conure sitting quietly and scraping the lower part of its beak against the top, don't worry. A lot of parrots do this when they are contented, sleepy, or just resting comfortably after a meal. While it may sound grating to your ears, it is a sign that your conure is relaxed and happy.

15. *Slowly rubbing the head against a toy, with fluffed feathers and eyes closed.* Some conures love to be petted so much that they will pet themselves with a toy or other object if no human is available.

16. *Pulling gently at your hair, eyelashes, eyebrows, beard, or mustache; licking or carefully nibbling your skin.* Called allopreening, this behavior is practiced in flocks of birds in the wild. You might also

Allopreening.

notice birds in pet stores preening each other, or see pet birds doing the same thing. This action serves several purposes, including removing dried feather sheaths after molting, conveying affection, and companionable grooming. If your conure preens your skin or hair, enjoy the special attention and then return the favor. Using your fingertips, gently tug your conure's head feathers. If it closes its eyes and zones out, you can be sure that it is enjoying the attention. But if it squawks and nips at you, you may have bumped a sensitive blood feather. Back up, give your little feathered companion a second to relax, then slowly resume the preening. This can be a very special time of bonding for you and your conure.

17. *Attacks or bites you when someone else gets too close.* In the wild, conures will often attempt to drive predators away by flying at them, screaming, or attacking. If this doesn't work, the conure will bite its mate to force it to retreat from danger. In captivity, the perceived danger may come from friends, family members, or strangers your conure dislikes. Instead of attacking the intruder, the conure may attempt to drive its mate (you) away from the perceived danger (the intruding humans). It may bite you, scream in your face, or chase you. Try to identify situations that stimulate this behavior and remove your conure from the situation before it goes into protect mode. Even a normally well-behaved, gentle conure can do serious damage to your face, head, or neck if it tries to drive you away from danger while perched on your shoulder. It's difficult to remember that your conure is only trying to protect you while it's shredding your ear.

18. *Preening.* If you see your conure going over each feather one at a time with its beak, it is grooming itself. This behavior will be performed enthusiastically after a bath, very frequently during the molt, and any time during the day if a feather gets out of place. Think of preening as being equivalent to combing your hair!

19. *Wing stretching.* Have you ever noticed your conure leaning slightly to the side, stretching one wing out as far as it will go, repeating the action with the other wing, and then shrugging both shoulders really high? If so, then you've witnessed a typical conure greeting. Many conures will stretch a greeting when their favorite human companion enters the room or approaches the cage.

20. *Sitting shakily with both feet on the perch, quivering feathers, closed or glassy-looking eyes.* A sick conure will shiver and fluff its feathers, may appear to have difficulty keeping its eyes open, and be unsteady on its perch. If you notice your conure doing this, contact your avian veterinarian immediately.

Baby Sun conures.

Juvenile Behavior and Appearance

Very young conures may not look as sleek and trim as adult birds because they haven't yet molted their juvenile feathers. It's common for baby conures to have broken tail feathers or rough-looking plumage until they go through their first molt.

Healthy hand-fed babies may cry for attention. If you're sure that your baby conure isn't hungry but it continues to cry, then it probably just wants to be played with or cuddled. A young, fully weaned conure may sometimes sit with its head back and beak open, all the while making pitiful sounds. If you're sure that your conure is okay and isn't hungry or hurt, don't overrespond to this behavior. That smart little conure could learn to cry any time it wants attention.

Very young conures will take frequent naps during the day. Upon waking they should be alert, bright eyed, and ready to play. They will often go through a "beaking" phase, where they want to explore everything by chewing, biting, or tasting. Distract your conure from biting by offering safe chew toys or other interesting diversions. If your baby bites often, don't respond with loud cries of pain because verbal responses can reinforce biting. Quickly offer a diversion, and get your finger out of reach!

Tip: Another way to discourage this behavior is to give your conure an exaggerated angry scowl or a heavy frown while saying *"No!"* in a forceful voice. This works well with some conures, and doesn't make the least impression on others! You might also try a short time-out in the cage to discourage your conure from biting. Pay attention to your conure's response to see which method works best with it.

Normal Adult Appearance and Behavior

A healthy adult conure should have smooth, shiny feathers, bright eyes, a good appetite, and a keen interest in day-to-day activities. When sleeping or resting, the conure will usually perch steadily with one foot tucked up into the fluffed-down feathers of the abdomen for warmth. A sleeping conure may also tuck its beak into the chest, neck, or back feathers to prevent heat loss. When awakened, a healthy adult conure will immediately be alert, bright eyed, and vocal. Any changes in your conure's normal behavior or appearance could signal illness.

Healthy adult Fiery-shouldered conure.

Problematic Behavior

Biting, screaming, and feather mutilation are problems that sometimes present in conures for a variety of reasons. Before attempting to modify any of these behaviors, first make sure that there are no medical reasons behind them. If your conure suddenly starts to pull out or chew feathers, to bite hard for no apparent reason, or starts to scream constantly, have your avian veterinarian schedule a checkup to make sure nothing is going on with your conure's health. Once health problems are ruled out, look into the conure's everyday habits, as well as those of the humans it lives with, and its diet and environment. Following are a few of the most common problems you may encounter:

Feather Picking, Plucking, or Chewing

Some conures develop the disagreeable habit of pulling out or damaging their feathers. There can be many reasons for this. Dirty or damaged feathers, not enough baths, boredom, poor diet, insufficient grooming, skin infections, not enough UV rays, disease, heavy metal toxicity, sexual maturity, missing their favorite human companion, or an infestation of mites can all cause a conure to start plucking or chewing its feathers. If your conure begins to exhibit this behavior, take it to an avian veterinarian as soon as possible to rule out any illness or disease.

If there are no health issues involved, the problem is probably behavioral. Try providing extra baths, lots of playtime and exercise, and fun new toys to shred and chew. If stress is the cause, try moving the cage to another, less busy location in the home. It might be helpful to put the cage near a large bird-safe plant so the conure can hide if it wants to. Find out if someone is teasing or scaring your conure and if that is the case, put a stop to it!

Devices such as collars are available to prevent feather plucking or chewing. These collars keep the conure from being able to reach the feathers. As uncomfortable as they may look, the collars can give new feathers a chance to grow in and the old, chewed ones to molt out.

Self-mutilation

While self-mutilation can be caused by boredom, other likely causes are poor diet or injury. Poor diet can cause itchy skin or rough feathering that irritates the conure and prompts it to tear feathers or gnaw at itself. An injury that might have started out as a slight scratch or cut could bother the conure to the point that it picks at the affected area until it becomes bloody and infected. If you notice any bloody spots or wounds on your conure, take it to your avian veterinarian immediately for a diagnosis and treatment.

The veterinarian may treat the mutilated spot with antibiotic ointments and prescribe oral antibiotics,

Smoking

If anyone in the home smokes, have them smoke outside and then wash their hands before handling your conure. Conures are very sensitive to nicotine, and nicotine on someone's hands can get on the conure's skin, causing discomfort and irritation. The conure might chew or pluck the feathers that have nicotine on them.

other medical preparations, or a change in diet. It is likely that your conure will have to wear a special collar designed to keep it from reaching the irritated places. The collar restricts the conure from further mutilation but doesn't interfere with its ability to eat or play.

Biting

A conure may bite for many reasons: fear, anger, jealousy, illness, or simply because it wants to provoke a response from a human. Under no circumstances should you thump a conure on the beak, slap it, or physically punish it in any way for biting. The only thing this will achieve will be to harm the conure and to frighten it. It may also learn to distrust you and the biting could become more severe.

To prevent painful bites, pay close attention to your conure's body language. Most conures will let you know a bite is imminent by squaring the head feathers, growling, or flashing the pupils. Some conures may make a hissing sound, or sit with an open beak. To avoid painful bites to your head, ears, or face, don't allow your conure to sit on your shoulder. Some conures become aggressive when sitting this high and can safely be allowed only on an arm or hand.

If the conure is perched on your hand or arm and you see that it is about to bite, jerk your arm slightly. This will throw your conure off balance and it will be too busy trying to regain its balance to bite. If your conure manages to get its beak dug into a finger or hand, push the conure away from you instead of jerking toward yourself. Again, the conure is forced off balance and it will have to let go. In a stern, sharp voice, say *"No!"* or *"No biting!"*

Reacting to a Screaming Conure

It's important not to scream or yell back at a conure when it is screeching. It will think that you are playing along, and will learn that screaming brings rewards. Don't rush to the cage every time your conure squawks, unless there is reason to believe something is wrong. If you respond by running to the conure, it will soon learn to scream whenever it wants your attention—it will be training you to respond to its commands! Sometimes ignoring a yelling conure can help discourage the noise. If it learns that no response is forthcoming, there will be less reason to yell.

The use of distractions and offering safe things to chew as alternatives to biting can be helpful. Sometimes, putting the conure back into its cage for a little time-out is useful. If the biting is behavioral, work to see what is causing the problem. Has someone been teasing it? Is anything stressing it out? Is it ill? If the problem suddenly develops in a conure that never had a habit of biting before, take it to see an avian veterinarian to rule out any health problems.

Screaming

A lot of parrots make noise at certain times of day, most usually at sunup and at sunset. By calling to each other and receiving responses, wild conures make sure that each flock member is safe and accounted for. This type of vocalization is normal, and even though they weren't raised in the wild, some pet conures do this, too. Many also scream whenever their favorite human flock member is out of sight. Sudden screams or earsplitting squawks can signal alarm, that something is wrong, or that the conure is frightened or hurt. Some conures also love to scream, screech, or squawk simply for the fun of it. Pay attention to your conure's vocalizations. Learn to discriminate between alarm calls and the noises made by a conure that is just happy to be alive.

If your conure develops a screaming problem, try to determine what prompts the noise. What is going on in the household at that

Include your conure in any interesting activity before it has a chance to start yelling.

time? Are there a lot of people or other pets moving around too closely to the conure's cage? Is everyone excited or rushing around getting ready for work or school? In these cases, a different placement of the cage inside the home may solve the problem.

A frightened conure has a piercing alarm scream—some of the larger conures can be almost as loud as Amazon parrots! The cause for alarm may simply be that a strange cat or dog is in the yard, or that an unfamil-iar human has crossed the conure's line of vision. A hawk, crow, or other large bird flying past the window is a major cause of alarm for most caged birds. Close the curtains or blinds until the perceived danger has passed.

If your conure squawks desper-ately whenever you leave the room, call softly to it to let it know where you are and encourage it to softly call back. Or place the cage so the conure can see you as you do what-ever it is that is taking you away from its vicinity. Do some of your daily chores within sight of the cage or playstand, such as folding laundry, putting away dishes, or dusting. Some conures love the sound of a vacuum cleaner and will dive head-first into their water cups for a bath. A conure that is bathing won't have time to scream.

If the conure screams during mealtimes, when the telephone rings, or when the television is on, there are a few options you can try. Allow the conure to join flock activities by giving it a small dish of whatever is on the dinner menu (remember the safety rules—no avocado, chocolate, alcohol, sugary, fried, or greasy foods), or by letting it play on the sofa while you're watching TV. Hand over a favorite treat when you're on the telephone, or encourage it to play with toys inside the cage. Make certain to include the conure in any interesting activity before the unacceptable noise starts.

For more stubborn noisemakers, try covering the cage with a dark towel or cage cover. If that doesn't help, it may be necessary to put the conure, cage and all, in a darkened room for a while. Don't forget to bring the conure back after it has been quiet for 10 or 15 minutes. The amount of noise generated by a conure is often directly related to the environment in which it lives. If the family is noisy, the conure will be noisy! Likewise, a conure will be quieter in a quieter household. If it seems that your conure makes much more noise than it should, it may be time to evaluate the environment and make some adjustments. Play radios and televisions at lower levels, don't shout from room to room, and try to reduce the noise levels in the home overall.

Other Factors That May Affect Conure Behavior

Stress

Stress in humans can cause headaches, illness, nervousness, sleep problems, and other uncomfortable reactions. But did you know that conures also react to stress? Things that may not bother you can be stressful for your conure. New furniture, visitors with whom your conure is unfamiliar, remodeling work that includes loud hammering or sawing, a new baby in the house, the sounds of construction work going on nearby, excessive traffic noises, sudden loud noises of any sort, teasing, new pets, or any significant changes in the conure's daily routine. A conure that is experiencing excessive stress might start screaming, seem fearful, lose its appetite, and become nervous.

Here are some signs that your conure may be stressed:

• *Watery droppings.* These will appear as very watery splotches in the bottom of the cage instead of the conure's normal droppings. The droppings should become firm again when the stressful situation has passed and the conure has calmed down. If you notice stress droppings, you might try relocating the cage to a quieter area of the home, or cover the cage for a bit to see if that helps.

• *Chewed feathers, picking, or plucking.* Some conures under stress will chew their feathers or pull them out. If your conure starts to damage its feathers, first have an avian veterinarian check it to make sure no physical problems exist. Try to discover what is stressing your conure, and alleviate the situation.

Boredom

Intelligent birds such as conures can become bored if all they ever do is sit in a cage day after day, with nothing to challenge their minds or occupy their time. A few signs that your conure is bored are
• Feather picking
• Excessive screaming
• Constant calling for attention
• Excessive masturbation

To alleviate boredom, offer lots of interesting toys, safe branches (with bark) to be shredded, tasty treats, or more time out of the cage. Train your conure to amuse itself by supplying it with plenty of its favorite items. Remember, these actions could also signify illness. If your conure suddenly begins to exhibit any of these behaviors, take it to the veterinarian to rule out health problems.

If your work schedule means that your conure will be alone for many hours each day, you can ease its boredom by making sure that there are always plenty of things for it to do while you are gone. Keep a supply of toilet paper rolls cut into short sections, single-serving-sized boxes of raisins, safe wooden chew toys, or swings for it to play with. A bird-safe metal mirror is fun for conures, and stainless steel bells with lead-free nonremovable clappers are favorites. Some conures enjoy chewing on white cotton ropes or clean strips of fabric tied in knots.

Sexual Maturity

Some conures experience behavioral changes when they become sexually mature, and some tame

This Mitred conure has plucked its chest, belly, and leg feathers.

Scooter's Sexual Maturity

Scooter, a gregarious Green-cheeked conure, lived in a bird store with his human companion, who had hand-fed him and cared for him from his first days. Scooter had everything a conure could possibly want—a large cage filled with every toy imaginable, a cozy sleeping bag, and all the treats and healthy foods he could eat.

He spent more time outside the cage than in, and enjoyed helping his human manage the store and bird-breeding facility. Scooter was the apple of his owner's eye, and was a very spoiled and pampered conure.

Then one day he began to bite, and bite hard. He pulled out some of his feathers, and didn't want to be held or played with. His owner, an experienced conure breeder, recognized the signs. Scooter was becoming sexually mature, and the urge to breed was taking over. She tried to coax Scooter to remain her pet by offering him even more new toys, and interesting, tasty treats. To her dismay, nothing worked.

Finally, the concerned and caring owner set Scooter up with a lovely little Green-cheeked female. The pair took to each other almost immediately, and before long went to nest. They produced many beautiful, healthy babies, and Scooter's human chose one to be her special pet. She was heartbroken to lose Scooter, but happy to see him enjoying his life not as a pet, but as a sexually mature, breeding conure.

conures may even lose their tameness and become unhappy being pets. Many sexually mature conures will masturbate by rubbing against a favorite toy, the cage bars, or a perch. Sometimes, your conure may back up to and rub against you. This is an indication that it thinks of you as its mate and sexual companion. A certain amount of masturbation is normal for most conures, but a frustrated or bored conure may masturbate to excess. To help avoid this behavior, provide plenty of distractions such as cotton rope toys to preen, safe chewable wooden toys, extra baths, and a well-balanced diet that includes lots of leafy green vegetables to shred.

The Shy Conure

Most conures for sale now are domestically bred hand-fed babies, but from time to time older, imported conures can still be found, and sometimes breeder conures are offered for sale. While it's understandable why conures like this may not be tame, sometimes even hand-fed babies lose their tameness for various reasons. With patience, understanding, and time, such conures can make wonderful pets.

It's easier to work with a conure if its wings are clipped, so have your avian veterinarian clip the wings, or do it yourself if you know how. Start working with a shy conure by making sure it feels safe and secure. It would be a good idea to put the cage in a quiet location with little traffic or household noise. Always speak softly when approaching the cage and don't make any sudden, unexpected moves. Let the conure know what you are doing at all times.

Proceed slowly with any actions; if you try to rush, you may only succeed in making the conure uncomfortable or nervous. Schedule several taming sessions a day, or simply spend a lot of time sitting beside the cage while you are reading or watching television. Be sure to stop any session or move quietly away if the conure appears frightened or stressed. The key is to go slowly, be persistent and gentle, and respect the conure's feelings. Let it adjust to being near you, and soon it will realize that you are a friend and mean it no harm.

During this period, offer lots of treats such as bits of apple, sunflower seeds, or other goodies. Encourage the conure to take the treats from your fingers. At first, it may grab the food and run away with it. Be persistent and keep offering the tidbits. Eventually, your conure will begin to accept the treats and will sit near you as it enjoys them. Remember, go slow, don't rush the conure, and be patient.

Taming Tips

• Once you're ready to start taking the conure out of its cage, begin working with it in a small room, such as a bathroom. First close the toilet, and empty the sink or bathtub to avoid accidents.

Treats can be helpful during training.

• Allow the conure out of its cage while you take a seat on the floor nearby. To keep the conure from retreating back inside the cage, be sure to close the cage door. If the conure seems too afraid and is trying to bite, let it walk around on the floor until it is more comfortable.
• Have a supply of its favorite treat handy, such as sunflower seeds or

Capturing a Conure Inside the Home

What if your new conure runs away inside the house and you have to catch it? It won't take you very long to discover just how quick these little parrots can be. Here's a simple way to catch your escapee: Close the curtains or blinds, or dim the room lights so that the conure can't see as well. Then gently drop a lightweight towel over it. Scoop up the conure, being careful not to get any of your own body parts within reach of the beak, and ease your captive back into the cage.

apple slices. Offer a treat and give the conure a chance to accept it. It may ignore the treat at first but if you are patient, it will eventually snatch a taste. Praise your conure lavishly and offer another goody. Getting it to accept food from your hand with no cage bars between you is a step in the right direction.

• Once you have managed to get the conure to take food from you, calmly work with it until you can get it to step up onto your hand or a perch. This can be scary with a nervous conure because you may be bitten. If you think the conure will bite, use a stick or small perch instead of your finger.

• Gently press the perch against the conure's belly and ask the bird to step up. Usually the conure will step up to avoid being pushed off-balance, but some may run away. Take your time, stay calm, and try again. Remember, it will more than likely take several sessions to get the conure to successfully step up, but some conures learn quickly. Don't get frustrated with the conure if it refuses to cooperate. Be patient, but persistent. Once the conure has stepped up as asked, reinforce the behavior until it consistently steps up on command. Reward it each time with its favorite treat.

It may take a while for the conure to allow you to handle it beyond this, or even to touch its feathers. By being patient, kind, and nonthreatening, eventually the conure will understand that you aren't going to hurt it and it will learn to trust you. Some conures tame quickly, but others may take months to become comfortable with being handled. Allow a shy conure as much time as it needs, and always respect its feelings.

Trick-Training

Young conures can be easier to trick-train than older birds, but conures of any age can learn to master simple tricks. Before you begin a training program, it's a good idea to clip your conure's wings. Flighted conures can be difficult to train since they have the ability to fly away if they don't wish to participate. Most conures are eager to join in on anything that seems like a game, and are quick to learn. Some

Peach-fronted conures.

even develop trick behaviors on their own.

Keep training sessions short. If either you or your conure begins to feel stressed, stop the session and try again later. It's important never to work with your conure if either one of you is tired, hungry, or in a bad mood. Your conure may pick up on your mood and react accordingly. Likewise, if the conure appears tired or loses interest, end the session and take it up again later.

Make sure the area you choose to train in is safe and nonthreatening, and that your conure feels comfortable. Always work in a location with few distractions. Turn off televisions and radios so the conure will focus on you. Remember to reward and praise your conure when it responds appropriately, and to make the training sessions fun. If a conure enjoys the training sessions, it will look forward to them and will learn much more quickly. Here are three fun, simple things to teach your conure:

1. *Shaking Hands.* Observe your conure's regular actions. Does it tend to pick up one foot whenever you approach? If so, you can turn this action into a trick behavior. To teach your conure to shake hands, gently grasp the raised foot and say, *"Shake hands!"* Before long, the conure will get the idea and will raise its foot when given the verbal command. Reinforce the behavior by giving the conure a treat each time it successfully completes the trick.

2. *Waving Good-bye.* It helps if your conure already knows how to

The Jenday conure.

shake hands, since this trick involves raising a foot. To teach your conure to wave good-bye, repeat the word *"Good-bye"* or *"Bye, bye,"* and then wave at the conure as it raises its foot. You may have to lift the conure's foot carefully and help it when you first start. You can even turn this into *"Gimme four!"* Again, reward the conure with a treat whenever it waves good-bye on command.

3. *The Toy Box Trick.* Find a small box and place several interesting little items inside. Given a conure's natural curiosity, it won't take long for it to want to see what's in the box. Demonstrate the trick by first removing an item and showing it to the conure. Then take out another

Using Words Appropriately

A Blue-crowned conure, Rio, a wild-caught bird, learned to say the words, *"Is it good?"* whenever he saw someone eating. To solicit a taste of the much-desired food, he would lean forward, flutter his wings, and repeat the phrase until a bit of the treat was handed over. One day, a member of his family entered the room carrying a pizza box. No one mentioned what was in the box, or opened the box in front of Rio. But the smart little bird knew what was going on. Immediately, he began asking, *"Is it good?"* over and over until a conure-sized slice of pizza was set in front of him!

item, and another, until the box is empty. One by one, replace the items in the box while your conure watches. By this time, your little feathered friend should be bursting with curiosity and will want to grab the toys and throw them out of the box. Show it how to pick up the items and then drop them back inside the box. It shouldn't take long for your conure to get the hang of things. As always, reward your conure when it performs the trick.

Props

Some companies sell props such as tiny basketball goals and basketballs, roller skates, and bird-sized cars. Training videotapes are also available. A conure that has mastered the toy box trick should be able to learn to dunk a birdie basketball!

Conures enjoy turning almost any activity into a game and can easily learn to use props. Just remember to end training sessions if you or your conure get bored or stressed. Pay attention to what it is doing while you are working with it. Be patient, and don't try to force the conure to do a trick or handle a prop if it isn't interested.

Clicker Training

Clicker training involves using a device to make a clicking sound when you want your conure to perform a desired action. Clickers can be found in pet stores, but you can use items found in your home, too. For example, the little lids that come on baby food jars make a clicking sound when the center is depressed. You might even click your tongue to get the right sound! It's important to note that some conures respond aggressively to clicking sounds, so you might want to choose an alternate sound that doesn't stimulate this behavior in your conure.

Use your chosen sound as positive reinforcement when your conure has performed an action correctly. Click while the action is being done, then reward your conure with a treat such as a raisin or sunflower seed. A bright conure will soon associate the behavior with the click, and will learn to perform a specific action when it hears the cue. Don't forget to offer a reward!

Talking

While not known to be as easily understandable as some of the larger parrots, conures can learn to speak, and some learn to speak clearly. Most conures can learn to say their names and a few words, while others develop moderate vocabularies. A conure's voice is usually not as human-sounding as that of a larger parrot, but can be lots of fun to listen to.

Patagonian conures, with their powerful voices, can sometimes mimic human speech very clearly. So can some talented Nanday conures, Red-fronted conures, Blue-crowned conures, and Sun conures. As long as you don't expect your conure to speak as clearly as an African grey or a yellow-naped Amazon, you won't be disappointed with its vocalizations. Work with it patiently, persistently, and often. Remember that some parrots never speak, even those with reputations for being excellent talkers.

Many conures learn to speak by associating a word or phrase with an action. Saying *"Night, night"* when covering the cage at night can help your conure learn to respond with those words. A conure trained in the *Up* command might say *"Up"* whenever you approach.

Pay attention to your enunciation. Conures will emulate the pronunciations and inflections they hear most often. You will sometimes be able to tell which person the conure is imitating by the inflections of its voice.

Young conures learn to speak more quickly than older birds.

To teach your conure to speak, first turn off televisions or radios, and put away any distracting items. Start by holding the conure up in front of your face and repeating the phrase you wish to teach. Speak clearly and slowly, and make sure that your conure is paying attention. An interested conure will focus on your lips, may tilt its head, or lean toward you. A bored conure will look around, try to climb down, or attempt to engage you in a game. If this happens, try again later. It might take several sessions before your conure attempts to speak, or it might surprise you by trying the words right away. It all depends on the individual conure.

Jenday conure.

First words: Some easy first words for conures are *"What?" "Hi" "No"* and *"Stop!"* Any words said with force are interesting to conures. But be careful what you say around your conure; like children, they tend to repeat what they hear whether or not it is appropriate, and usually in front of company.

Association: Association is a good way to teach your conure appropriate speech. Hand over a favorite treat, such as a bit of apple, and clearly repeat the word "apple."

It won't take a smart conure long to associate the word with the food, and before long you may be pleasantly surprised to hear your feathered friend saying "apple" as soon as the treat appears.

Note: Keep in mind that not every conure will speak, no matter how long or hard you work with it.

Various sounds: Whistling, singing, household noises, the sounds of certain bodily functions, exaggerated kissing sounds, and other pet or animal vocalizations are all fun for conures. Some can learn to bark or meow very well, and may even learn to call the dog or cat. Conures have been known to scold the family pet, or to tattle on human children. Some conures never develop clear speaking voices, but may mimic the cadence and tone of certain humans so well that there is no question which family member they are copying.

Tapes: Video- and cassette tapes are available that help teach birds to talk. While interacting one on one with your conure is the best way to teach it to speak, these tapes might be useful. Hearing other parrots speaking may stimulate your conure to try a new word or two. These teaching aids can be found in pet stores, ordered from Internet avian supply companies, and from advertisements in the backs of bird magazines. Just remember that these things will never take the place of personal interaction between you and your conure.

Chapter Nine
Part of the Family

Before you know it, that shy little conure you adopted will have taken over the household and become a full-fledged member of the family. As with any special family member, you'll want to include it in your celebrations, holidays, vacations, and even things as simple as television time. With a bit of thoughtful planning, your conure will be able to join in on all the activities.

Celebrating the Holidays Safely

It's fun to deck the halls during the holidays, and if your home contains a conure, you can still get into the spirit of things. You just have to be extra careful to use only conure-safe items. While a great many home decorations are nontoxic, others are not, and there is the danger of gastrointestinal distress, impaction, or death if a conure eats them.

Those pretty bubbling Christmas tree lights contain methylene chloride, which is a very toxic solvent. Don't let your conure have access to them! Also make sure to keep all electrical cords and strings of electric lights out of reach, as well as any batteries. And if you're going to be using fragile glass ornaments, don't let your conure play with them. It would take only a tiny piece of shattered glass to cause severe harm, or to kill a conure. Ingested tinsel could wrap around intestines, ornaments containing any amounts of lead can be deadly, and artificial snow would be extremely attractive to an inquisitive conure. Keep poinsettias, holly berries, mistletoe, wreaths, and other holiday plants out of reach because these items can cause toxic reactions in conures. In short, it's safest to keep your conure away from *all* holiday decorations and plants. Let it admire your beautiful things from a distance.

Candles and Potpourri

Candles are important parts of many holiday observances, and if your celebrations include candles, you can safely use them as long as you take a few precautions. Unscented candles, candles made of beeswax, and soy candles scented

A festive Sun conure.

with natural essential oils will be safe to use in the same room with your conure if you keep the items out of reach. The beautiful flickering flames will attract the curiosity of a nosy conure that may decide it just has to reach out and see what the pretty, bright things are. To avoid serious burns to your conure, keep any candles out of reach. And of course, you'll want to make sure your conure can't accidentally knock over a burning candle and start a fire. Restrict your conure to another room of the house (with a few special treats so that it doesn't feel left out) when you will be using your candles. Or, if you wish to keep your conure near during the celebrations, be sure to keep it locked securely inside its cage while the candles are lit.

During the holiday season you may be tempted to use heavily scented candles and potpourri. Unfortunately, these things can cause marked avian respiratory distress and irritation to your conure's eyes or nose. Scented candles, air fresheners, potpourri, and other holiday home scents contain volatile oils, various chemicals, and fragrances.

For the sake of your conure's health, try scenting your home by simmering cinnamon sticks and cloves, a vanilla bean, or a fresh-smelling mixture of citrus peels and spices in hot water. Remember, do not use a nonstick pan because the fumes from the pans can kill conures. If you still want to use holiday scented candles or air fresheners, don't use them in the same room as

your conure. Be sure to adequately vent the room in which the candles or air fresheners are in use. And, of course, never allow your conure to have access to burning candles, or to eat the melted candle wax or pot-pourri mixture.

Conure-Safe Gift Wrapping

Gift giving is a fun part of any holiday or birthday celebration. Who doesn't like to receive a present wrapped up in pretty paper and topped off with a bow? Feel free to wrap gifts for your human family members in shiny foil gift paper, but keep all foil papers out of the reach of interested beaks. If a conure eats any of that attractive foil paper, it could suffer an intestinal blockage or severe tummy distress, and heavily colored papers could contain harmful inks, so don't let your conure eat those, either.

When selecting gifts for the family, don't leave your conure off the list. Conures enjoy getting presents, too! Just remember to wrap any birdy gifts in plain paper, flattened sections of brown paper bags, blank newsprint, or typing paper. Your conure won't mind what the package looks like, as long as ripping the paper to shreds is part of the deal!

Three Great Conure Gift Ideas

Want to give your conure a special holiday gift? Here are a few fun suggestions:

1. *Colorful wooden chew sticks.* These sticks come in pretty hues that are safely done with nontoxic vegetable dyes. Not only do they make great foot toys, but conures adore chewing them to bits. And because these intelligent birds can see colors, don't be surprised if your conure demonstrates a preference for a certain color.

2. *Untreated rawhide or leather toys.* Because treated items can contain unsafe chemicals or tanning agents, be sure to purchase only untreated leather or rawhide toys. Read the package to see if the item is safe, or check with the store clerk. Your conure will enjoy trying to tear up these tough toys. Just make sure to dispose of any leather or rawhide that finds its way into the water cup. Wet leather or rawhide can't be sterilized and will become fertile breeding grounds for harmful bacteria and germs.

3. *Clean pinecones.* Your conure will have a blast destroying the soft woody fibers! If you don't have access to fresh pinecones, there are several companies that sell pinecone toys that are stuffed with seeds, nuts, or bits of fruit. Ask at your favorite pet store, or order one from an on-line bird supply company. If you gather your own pinecones, make sure there is no dirt or debris on them, that they are free of mold, and that there are no insects hiding anywhere inside. To minimize the risk of disease transmission from outside birds and animals, rinse the pinecones thoroughly, then bake in an oven on a low setting until dry.

Party Time

Everyone has a party or family gathering at one time or another. While these occasions can be great fun for an outgoing, gregarious conure, they can be overly stressful for a shy one. But even if your conure is the nervous kind, you can still enjoy having people over.

A timid conure will be happier if it is removed from the action before it has a chance to feel stressed. Take it to another room before your guests begin arriving. Keep the door closed and let everyone know not to disturb your conure. You might consider posting a polite sign on

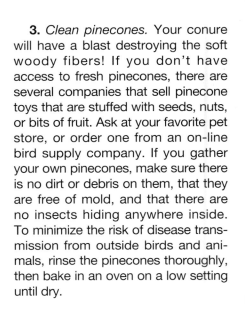

Conures love toys!

This Green-cheeked conure is enjoying a bit of cinnamon toast.

the door, or even locking it. This way, children, or anyone who may not be aware of the situation, won't accidentally barge in. Make sure to give your conure some special treats, and check on it often during the evening. You may even want to cover its cage early.

If your conure is a party bird and will be joining your guests, be certain that you will be able to supervise all interactions. It would be too easy for someone to innocently slip your conure a dangerous treat such as avocado, chocolate, caffeine, or alcohol. To prevent that from happening, don't serve any of these foods, or bring them out only after you have put the conure to bed.

For special treats that can be enjoyed by everyone, serve foods that can be safely shared such as a vegetable or fruit tray, a plate of crackers and cheese, or a bowl of

unsalted, unbuttered popcorn intended especially for your conure. After everyone has had a chance to interact, whisk your conure away to a quiet room. Too much attention and exposure to people with whom your conure may not be familiar can stress even the friendliest bird.

Traveling with Conures

Many people enjoy taking their conures on family trips with them. More and more hotels are allowing pets, so call ahead to find places that will welcome your feathered companion. Often, a small deposit will be required. Always take along a cage cover to help your conure sleep in a strange place, and plenty of newspapers or sheets to cover the area surrounding the cage.

Maintain your conure's regular diet while traveling.

Before leaving on any trip with your conure, pack up a generous supply of its regular foods, a few bottles of drinking water, a spray bottle of water, and some favorite toys. Never leave home without your avian first aid kit, and don't forget to take along a current health certificate from your conure's veterinarian. This document is necessary for traveling across any borders. It also would be a good idea to make sure your conure's wings are freshly clipped before leaving.

Safety Inside the Vehicle

Specially designed bird travel carriers are handy for taking the family conure along on trips. Always confine your conure to its travel cage or carrier when on the road. Not only does the carrier protect your conure, but a conure loose in the vehicle could cause an accident by flying in front of the driver or by causing other distractions. Your conure could also be injured or killed by slamming doors, electric windows going up or down, falling out of the vehicle, or by being crushed when someone sits on it. When in a moving vehicle, the safest place for your conure to be is securely inside its carrier.

Always seat-belt or fasten the carrier in place. An unsecured carrier would be tossed around inside a vehicle during an accident, or after a sudden stop. And never place your conure in front of an air bag. Parrots have died from inflating air bags that crushed them and their cages.

If your conure will be traveling in a regular cage instead of a carrier, try to find a small one. The less room your conure has to flap or climb around, the better. Remove any toys, swings, or loose cups from the cage before placing it in the car. You don't want your conure to be injured by anything crashing around inside the cage. Place a perch securely in the lower part of the cage, or remove it and let your conure ride on a towel in the bottom of the cage. An elevated perch could be dangerous because your conure might be thrown from it during an accident or sudden stop.

You don't want a cup of water sloshing around in the cage or carrier, but you do need to take precautions that your conure doesn't get thirsty. A few pieces of moist fruit, such as orange slices or apple chunks, can be placed in the bottom of the carrier. This will keep your conure from getting dehydrated until you can fill its water cup. It's a good idea to also pack a spray bottle of water for bathing or cooling showers. In case your conure wants a snack, sprinkle some of its favorite pellets or seeds on the bottom of the carrier so it can nibble if it wants to.

Here are a few more tips for safe traveling with a conure:

• Be careful not to let your conure become overheated. Drape a towel over the cage to keep out direct sunlight, and monitor the temperature inside the vehicle.

• *Never* leave your conure unattended in a vehicle because the temperatures inside can change rapidly and the extremes could kill it. If you want to stop for a meal, arrange for one member of the family to wait in the vehicle with the conure so that temperatures can be constantly monitored.

• In cold weather, always warm up the vehicle before bringing your conure inside. You don't want to take the chance that it will get chilled.

• Some conures suffer from motion sickness. If your conure doesn't travel well, bring along a towel or cage cover to drape over the carrier. The darkness will help calm a nervous conure, and make it feel more secure.

Make sure your conure's wings are clipped before leaving home.

• Don't situate the carrier directly in line with a heating or cooling vent.

• Check on your conure frequently during the trip to reassure it and to make sure that everything is well.

Possible Hazards to Your Conure While on the Road

Even after you've taken all possible safety precautions, unforseen accidents can still occur. An active, headstrong conure can find all sorts of ways to get into trouble. Some things to watch out for are

• *Injuries.* Of course, your conure will choose this time to hurt itself on a toy, or get its head stuck in something. When your conure is out of

Travel Carriers

To find a travel carrier, drop by your favorite pet or bird store. Ask the store personnel to demonstrate how each model works, and to explain which carrier will be the best for your conure. You'll want one that allows for plenty of head and tail feather room, has safe, secure sides, adequate ventilation, and an opening that is large enough to comfortably let your conure in and out. Carriers are made from a variety of materials, such as acrylic, ABS plastic, wire, wood, or a combination of materials. Some carriers are made of clear material that allows you to see in, and your conure to see out. There are collapsible carriers that fold down flat for storage, and other models that come with covers to protect the birds inside from the weather. You can also use some roomy carriers as vacation or sleep cages when you reach your destination.

the travel cage or carrier, keep it in sight every second. A curious conure will have to explore every inch of the vehicle or hotel room, and will immediately find everything it shouldn't touch. Have your avian first aid kit within easy reach at all times.

• *Escape.* Be especially vigilant when any doors or windows are open. When your conure is playing outside of the carrier or cage, it would take only an instant for it to flutter or fly out of an opening. It can be difficult to recapture a runaway conure at home, but in an unfamiliar place it can be next to impossible. See that everyone is aware of the conure's whereabouts before opening any windows or doors.

Important: Make sure to clip your conure's wings before leaving home.

• *Other animals.* Don't leave your conure unattended at any time! You may be tempted to take your conure outside at a rest stop or campground and leave it sitting on a picnic table while you go for a walk. This is a bad idea, for many reasons. Other people's pets might attempt to get at the noisy little bird sitting unprotected inside its carrier, and knock it off the table. A wild animal would think nothing of attacking your conure, with possibly tragic consequences. It wouldn't be wise to take your conure out of its carrier to let it sit on your shoulder, either. A hawk could swoop down and snatch it, or it might fall off your shoulder and be grabbed by a passing dog or cat.

• *Theft.* Another good reason to never leave your conure unattended is the very real possibility of theft. Think how awful it would be if someone drove away with your conure! If you plan to stop for any reason, make sure someone will be with the conure every second.

Aside from physical accidents, there is the possibility of encountering diseases and illnesses such as Exotic Newcastle disease in affected areas. To protect your conure from various diseases, don't let it come in contact with wild bird droppings, or with unfamiliar pet birds. Because West Nile virus is spread by mosquito bites, keep your conure safe by staying indoors while in infested areas.

Don't leave home without the telephone numbers of reliable avian veterinarians at your fingertips. To find out what avian veterinarians are available in the areas you'll be visiting, contact the Association of Avian Veterinarians. You can visit their web site at *http://www.aav.org/aav.*

Leaving Your Conure at Home

Maybe you've decided not to take your conure along on the trip after all. So what do you do with it while you're on the road? Don't panic— you don't have to give up your travel plans. There are ways to see that your conure is well taken care of while you're away. Here are some ideas:

• *Board your conure at a pet shop, or with an avian veterinarian.* Not all these facilities provide boarding, but many do. If they don't board pets, ask them to recommend reliable boarding facilities.

• *Pet boarding facilities.* There are special facilities that are equipped to board different types of pets, conures included. Ask for references from veterinarians or other bird owners to find out which ones they trust.

Peach-fronted conure.

Visit the facility you are interested in to see if it is clean, safe, and staffed by knowledgeable, caring people who are pet owners themselves.

• *Personal pet-sitters.* These are folks who come into your home to provide care for your pets while you are away. Look in the yellow pages for pet-sitters, or ask other conure owners who they use. Before you hire a pet-sitter, get references from reliable sources and check them out. If there were any complaints, investigate them before hiring that particular person. If everything checks out, set up a time for the sitter to visit and meet your conure. Explain what its feeding schedule is and where its foods are kept, as well as any special

Ask the pet-sitter to closely supervise all play times.

instructions you may have. Try to find someone who is comfortable with birds and who will not be afraid to handle your conure if necessary. Make sure the sitter will be vigilant in cleaning the cage and cups, and will follow your wishes to the letter.

• *Friends and relatives.* These are people with whom your conure is probably already familiar. Choose someone who likes your conure, understands how to care for it, and is willing to come over *every* day to feed, water, talk to, and check on your bird.

Bird Shows and Fairs

Many bird clubs put on shows and exhibitions several times a year. Check your local newspapers or subscribe to bird club newsletters for schedules and information. Members of the clubs show their prize birds and sometimes sell hand-fed babies or breeder pairs. And attending a bird show can be a great opportunity to see conures you may have only read about.

You can exhibit your own conure, too. If you're interested in showing your conure, join a conure club to learn about the rules and regulations. You'll have to learn how to groom your conure for a show, as well as what kinds of cages are required for showing.

Caution: Be aware that taking your conure to a bird club meeting or show will expose it to any diseases that other birds present may have.

Bird fairs are like flea markets that display huge amounts of bird-related items. Cages, toys, food, nest boxes, books, accessories, even bird-shaped jewelry and clothing decorated with birds are sold. Usually there will be several booths set up with various species of birds for sale, and many people take their own birds with them when they visit the fairs. While this can be a fun chance to show off your conure, understand that if any of the birds there are ill, your conure could catch a disease from them. It's usually better to enjoy the show on your own and tell your conure all about it when you get home.

After you've visited a bird show or fair, and especially if you've handled any of the birds, shower and change your clothes as soon as you get home. If you pick up your conure before doing so, you risk exposing it to any germs or bacteria that may be on your hands or clothes.

Giving Up Responsibly

What if after all your research, hard work, and care, you discover that you and your conure are miserable together? If you've really tried to develop a relationship but failed, don't feel too bad. These feisty, energetic, noisy little parrots aren't for everybody. If you want to give up your conure, there are several options to consider.

• *Bird clubs.* Call them and explain the situation. If there isn't someone in the club who is willing to take your conure, it's possible that they can find someone who will.

• *People who already have birds.* Many bird lovers are happy to adopt

An attractive Green-cheeked conure.

"just one more." If you find someone who is willing to take your conure, be open and honest with why you're giving it up. Let that person know if the conure is extremely noisy, bites, has any other behavioral problems, or has health issues. You want your conure to be welcome in its new home, and you certainly don't want to put it in a situation where it will be given up again.

• *Bird rescues.* Call your veterinarian or animal shelter to find out if there is such a facility in your area.

• *Humane societies and animal shelters.* Call your local animal shelter or humane society and find out if they accept birds. If they don't, they

A conure is a wonderful companion for the right person.

might be able to refer you to a shelter that will. Then visit the facility to make sure it will be a suitable place for your conure.

• *Newspaper advertisements.* If you decide to run an ad, make sure to meet the person responding and speak with them about your conure. Determine that they are ready and able to accept the responsibility of caring for one of these busy, bossy little birds.

What Not to Do

It is *never* an acceptable option to abandon your conure outside. A pet conure is not equipped to fend for itself. It will be at the mercy of predators such as cats, hawks, dogs, foxes, and other animals. It might be hit by a vehicle, starve to death, or be poisoned. It will be at the mercy of the weather, and will be forced to search for food and safe shelter. A conure that was once a pet has no idea how to survive outdoors. If you decide to give up your conure, do so responsibly. Keep its welfare first and foremost in your mind. Remember, that little bird may be just the conure that someone else is searching for.

Glossary

Please note that the following definitions set forth the meanings of these words as they are used specifically in this text. They are not intended to be full and complete definitions.

Aggression   Describing the action of a conure that chases or tries to bite its human companions or other birds.

Allopreening   The act of preening a flockmate. A tame conure will preen its human companion by grooming the facial hair or skin. One way humans can reciprocate is by carefully scratching away dried feather sheaths from blood feathers.

Arboreal termites   Tree-dwelling termites.

Avian veterinarian   A doctor who specializes in treating birds.

Aviculture   Ornithology, or the study of birds, usually the keeping of birds; avian husbandry.

Beaking   Behavior demonstrated by some baby conures when learning to use their beaks; involves biting or chewing new and unfamiliar items, including human skin.

Blood feathers   New feathers that grow in during a molt. These feathers are covered with a keratin sheath, and a blood supply runs through them. They will bleed if broken.

Cage covers   Cloth coverings that are placed over the cage at night.

Clicker training   Training method involving the use of a clicker or other device to make a sound that will cue the conure to perform an action.

Cloaca   The area from which feces or eggs leave the body; also called the vent.

Conure bleeding disorder   A blood-clotting disorder thought to be caused by a vitamin K deficiency; also called CBS.

Crop   The place where the conure's food is stored prior to digestion; similar to a human's stomach.

Crop burns   Painful injuries that result from feeding a conure foods that are too hot.

Crown   The top of the head.

Deforestation   The cutting down of forests to create agricultural or residential areas.

Dietary supplements   Manufactured vitamins, powdered or liquid, that are added to a conure's diet. Other supplements include

Before long, your new conure will feel right at home.

minerals, calcium, probiotics, essential fatty acids, etc.

Down feathers   The fluffy soft feathers that lie closest to the skin.

Droppings   Feces and urine.

Egg binding   The condition that results when an egg isn't expelled from the female bird, but stays inside instead; can be life-threatening if the egg isn't removed.

Extruded foods   Processed bird foods.

Feather picking   The act of a conure pulling out, chewing, or otherwise damaging its own feathers.

Feather sheath   The translucent material that covers new feathers or pin feathers; will be a whitish color over dark blue.

Flappers   Conures that like to hang onto the sides of their cages and energetically flap their wings.

Flight feathers   The longest wing feathers; found at the outer edges of the wings.

Genus   Group of animals or plants with common characteristics.

Impaction   A blockage of the crop or intestines. The condition can be fatal if not relieved.

Flock   In the wild, a group of birds that live together. For pet conures, flock refers to the humans, other birds, or pets sharing its home.

Hand-fed   Describes a baby conure that was fed by humans instead of by the parent birds.

Health certificate   Paper showing that the conure has been examined by an avian veterinarian.

Health guarantee   A promise that your newly purchased conure is healthy; usually extends from 24–72 hours.

Hookbills   Parrots; refers to the curved, notched upper beak.

Hospital cage   An enclosure designed to temporarily house a sick conure.

Hybrids   The result of crossbreeding birds of different species.

Imports   Conures that were brought into the country from their native habitats.

Keel bone   The long bone that runs down the front of the chest.

Leg bands   Plastic or metal bands placed on the legs of conures for identification purposes.

Lores   The area above the nostrils.

Mandible   The beak.

Maxilla The upper part of the beak.

Microchip A tiny computer chip containing identifying information that is implanted inside a conure.

Molt The normal shedding of old feathers to be replaced by new ones.

Mutations Variations in coloring that occurs naturally in a species.

Nape The back of the neck.

Necropsy An autopsy.

Pasteurella bacteria Toxic bacteria found in cat claws and saliva.

Pellets Cylindrically shaped processed foods.

Periophtalmic eye rings Featherless rings of skin around the eyes.

Pet-sitter A person who comes to your home to care for your pets while you are away.

Playstands, playgyms Manufactured play areas outfitted with perches, cups, toy hangers.

Polytetraflouethylene (PTFE) A chemical used to coat nonstick cookware and other items.

Powder coat A sprayed-on finish used on cages that is rust-proof and bird-safe.

Preening The act of grooming the feathers.

Primary feathers The flight feathers.

Processed foods Pelleted diets or extruded foods for birds.

Props Small items used for tricks, such as tiny roller skates or bird-sized basketball goals.

Psittacines Parrots.

Quarantine The period of time when a new bird is sequestered

The Maroon-bellied conure.

from other birds in order to prevent the spreading of disease.

Regurgitation The act of bringing up partially digested food to be fed to the young or a mate. Sexually mature and bonded conures may regurgitate to their human companions.

Seed moths Tiny insects sometimes found in bags of birdseed; larval or adult moths may be seen.

Correct wing clipping does not harm conures.

Self-mutilation When a conure intentionally injures itself.

Sexually dimorphic Visually distinguishable between the sexes.

Silver nitrate sticks Substances used to stop the bleeding from an injured toenail; available from the veterinarian.

Species Groups of animals or plants within a genus.

Stress droppings Watery droppings caused by stress; not to be confused with diarrhea, which can be a sign of illness; clears up when the stress has passed.

Styptic powder A material used to help clot blood from broken toenails or blood feathers.

Subspecies Variations within a species.

Sympathy purchase Buying a sick or otherwise unsound conure because you feel sorry for it.

Tail bobbing A noticeable up-and-down motion of the tail caused by respiratory distress.

Theobromine A dangerous chemical found in chocolate.

Toxins Poisons.

Travel carrier A specially designed container for transporting birds.

Urates The solid urine components in a conure's droppings.

UV light Ultraviolet light; the healthy rays in sunshine or in certain purchased lighting fixtures.

Vent The area from which the feces or eggs are expelled; also called the cloaca.

Vitamin A deficiency A serious condition caused by poor diet; can lead to diseases, illness, poor feathering, and other significant health conditions.

Weaned Describes a young conure that no longer requires feeding by a parent bird or human, and is eating on its own.

Wing clipping The painless process of trimming the long flight feathers so that a conure's ability to fly is restricted.

Zygodactylous Like a parrot's foot, with two forward-pointing toes and two backward-pointing toes.

A Sharp-tailed conure.

Resources

Organizations
American Federation of Aviculture
P.O. Box 56218
Phoenix, AZ 85079

Association of Avian Veterinarians
P.O. Box 811720
Boca Raton, FL 33481

Bird Clubs of America
P.O. Box 2005
Yorktown, VA 23692

International Conure Association
P.O. Box 70123
Las Vegas, NV 89170
http://www3.upatsix.com/ica/

Pyrrhura Breeders Association
150 Road W
Hartford, KS 66854
*http://www.pyrrhurabreeders
    association.com*

Periodicals
Bird Talk Magazine
Fancy Publications, Inc.
P.O. Box 6050
Mission Viejo, CA 92690

Bird Times
Pet Publishing, Inc.
7-L Dundas Circle
Greensboro, NC 27407

Birds U.S.A.
Fancy Publications, Inc.
P.O. Box 6050
Mission Viejo, CA 92690

Companion Parrot Quarterly
P.O. Box 2428
Alameda, CA 94501

Books
Vriends, Matthew M., Ph.D.
Conures. Hauppauge, NY:
Barron's Educational Series, Inc.,
    2000.

Athan, Mattie Sue
*Guide to Companion Parrot
    Behavior.* Hauppauge, NY:
Barron's Educational Series, Inc.,
    1999.

Athan, Mattie Sue
*Guide to a Well-Behaved Parrot,
    Second Edition.*
Hauppauge, NY:
Barron's Educational Series, Inc.,
    1999.

Index

The White-eared conure.

Nanday conure.